Spring Creek Strategies

Spring Creek Strategies
HATCHES, PATTERNS, AND TECHNIQUES

MIKE HECK

Photographs by Jay Nichols

HeadWater
Books

STACKPOLE
BOOKS

Copyright © 2008 by Headwater Books

Published by
HEADWATER BOOKS
531 Harding Street
New Cumberland, PA 17070
www.headwaterbooks.com

STACKPOLE BOOKS
5067 Ritter Road
Mechanicsburg, PA 17055
www.stackpolebooks.com

Printed in China

First edition

10 9 8 7 6 5 4 3 2 1

ISBN: 978-0-9793460-4-0

Photography by Jay Nichols except where noted

Library of Congress Control Number: 2008922046

To my wife, Shelley, who has always been there for me as a wife, friend, and proofreader of everything I have written, from my first article to this book. I am blessed to have such a wonderful and caring wife. To my daughter, Breanne, whose smile is like sunshine on a warm spring day.

Contents

Acknowledgments

Thanks to my mom and dad for instilling in me values of trust, kindness, and a heartfelt love for the outdoors. Thanks also to my brother Brad for his support and one-liners, and to all of the fly fishermen, both clients and friends, who have fished these streams with me. Thanks to Jay Nichols for asking me to write this book. I was standing on the banks of a spring creek when I took Jay's call, and that seemed like a good omen for the project. For additional photo support, thanks to my good friend and accomplished fly fisherman Joe Tregaskes, to Jack Hanrahan for his breathtaking images of Pennsylvania spring creeks, and to John Randolph from *Fly Fisherman* magazine for contributing his shots of some of the famous spring creeks in Montana's Paradise Valley.

Every spring creek has its own character and secrets. Learn to catch trout in its clear currents, and you will most likely be able to catch trout anywhere in the world.

JACK HANRAHAN PHOTO

Introduction

Clear, cold spring creeks flow everywhere in the valleys around my hometown of Fayetteville, Pennsylvania, and I fell in love with them early. My parents would drop me off on the Falling Spring Branch and leave me for most of the day to fish. The clear waters were hard to fish, and it took me almost a year before I caught my first Falling Spring rainbow. I did just about everything wrong. But I learned from my mistakes, and as I kept working on my skills, I discovered different stream techniques that proved effective for the tough trout. After my Uncle Jim taught me how to tie my first fly, I began to collect insects and blend furs to match the live insects. As my techniques and patterns improved, so did my success rate.

Of all the spring creeks, Falling Spring Branch was my favorite as a kid, and it is still my favorite today. Although there are many great streams across the country—and many terrific spring creeks—no water has given me more than my home water. The challenges of Falling Spring fueled my desire to become a better fly fisherman and fly tier and made me want to guide, instruct, and help restore the streams I have fished over the years.

I don't claim to know all the answers for mastering spring creeks. Every creek has its individual character and secrets. It has taken me almost thirty years to begin to feel like I understand all of the complexities of my home water. But in this book I hope to share techniques to catch difficult fish under the most demanding conditions, which I have taught my clients with good success. I have been so lucky to have fished with fly anglers from around the world. I have shown my techniques and patterns to those I have fished with, and these fly anglers have been able to use these techniques and patterns on their own streams. And because of their beauty and challenges, the spring creeks draw these anglers back time and time again.

I'll share with you the fly patterns that I prefer to use (by no means the only ones that are effective), my favorite methods of presenting flies, and my thoughts on stealth and approach, which I consider key elements for success. In this book, I don't delve too much into casting or equipment. Equipment, such as length of rod or line weight, can be a personal choice based on a variety of conditions, and many good books already cover this ground thoroughly. If you're just beginning, you'll discover that fly fishing can be an equipment-intensive sport, but as you improve, you'll quickly learn to eliminate any gear that becomes a hindrance to helping you catch fish. If you've been fishing for a long time, you probably are already set in your ways regarding equipment. I do weigh in on leader design, which I think is a critical and often-overlooked aspect of successful fishing.

Casting is another one of those personal choices, and there are lots of great instructional materials out there to teach you the basic casts. I touch on a few casting techniques that I use most frequently, but I urge you to get lessons and work on your

To consistently catch fish in spring creeks, stealth and observation are your best tools. Learning to cast accurately in close quarters helps, too.

The plentiful aquatic vegetation in a healthy spring creek is both a blessing and a curse. Though it is home to insects on which trout feed, it also creates complicated surface currents to foil your presentations.

casting. If you had to prioritize your casting practice time, I recommend spending the most time developing your presentation casts rather than working on distance casting. For most spring creek fishing, time spent honing your slack-line casts and your ability to cast in tight quarters will pay off.

Though I have refined and practiced these techniques on my home waters, I have fared well with them on spring creeks across the country. Although each stream has its own character and unique set of challenges, many spring creeks have lots of similarities. I focus on these similarities in this book. The techniques in this book will help you become a

better angler on spring creeks, and once you can catch trout on these streams, you ought to be able to fish with confidence on any water, be it a spring creek, freestone stream, or tailwater.

Many great books have been written about spring creeks, and my book is intended as a humble contribution to spring-creek-tactics literature, focused primarily on Eastern spring creeks. However, information in this book may help you anywhere you fish, because in my opinion—and that of many other well-traveled anglers—these Eastern creeks can be some of the hardest waters in which to consistently catch fish.

CHAPTER 1

Big Fishing Creek, near Lamar, Pennsylvania, blurs the lines between freestone stream and limestone spring creek. Though it is spring-fed and runs through limestone geology, when it flows through "The Narrows" (above) it looks like a classic freestone stream.

Spring Creeks

To begin to understand what makes spring creeks so special, it often helps to first understand what they are not. Because almost every angler is familiar with freestone streams (they are the most common), I'll describe some of their characteristics first. The difference between a spring creek and a freestone river can be dramatic, and understanding that difference will help you ... ... creeks are. As you ...

... tains ... t and ... rough the year ... ... , freestone streams can get warm, and many ... dry up. Freestone streams mostly flow across shale, sandstone, and other rock formations that lack calcium carbonate, which would naturally reduce acidity in the water. So, some freestone streams may suffer from acid problems because of manmade factors such as mining and acid rain, or other natural factors such as tannins and other acidic, naturally occurring compounds leeching out of the soil. Acidic conditions (most freestone streams that do not have a limestone influence range from 6 to 4 in pH) do not favor growth of weeds or abundant fish and insect life.

Freestone streams have a wide range of insect and fish species and can have good trout populations, but during warmer weather the fish must travel to find cool springs and other thermal refuges. During hot, dry summers, freestone streams can become too warm, and catching and playing fish in the high water temperatures stresses them. After heavy rains, freestone streams do not clear as quickly as spring creeks. Lacking a clear groundwater source, and generally formed by smaller streams (tributaries), a freestone stream takes more time to clear from the debris and dirt associated with heavy rainfall.

Some freestone streams have spring creeks that dump into them and cool the water, increase pH, and create conditions for better insect hatches. A freestone stream with a large enough spring creek influence can resemble a spring creek, such as part of the Little Juniata River or the catch-and-release section of the Yellow Breeches, which are Pennsylvania freestone streams cooled by springs. Bald Eagle Creek is a good example of what large amounts of spring water can do for a stream. It starts out as a freestone stream, but as Bald Eagle Creek collects more spring water, it begins to take on the characteristics of a spring creek. The cool water encourages good hatches and abundant trout, and that portion of the stream fishes well even during hot summers. The Yellowstone River in Montana is another prime example of a stream with strong spring creek influences.

Spring Creeks

In the grand scheme of things, spring creeks are rare and make up only a fraction of the trout streams around the world, but where I live in southcentral Pennsylvania, we are blessed with an abundance of them. Part of a limestone belt that starts in Virginia

and runs into Maryland, Pennsylvania is one of the most fertile, spring-creek-rich areas in the world. Letort Spring Run, Big Spring Creek, Falling Spring Branch, and a host of others in southcentral Pennsylvania, and Spruce and Spring Creek in central Pennsylvania are but a few of the many spring creeks in the area. These waters were home to many of our sport's greatest anglers, fly tiers, and writers, spurring people like Vince Marinaro, Charlie Fox, Ed Shenk, Ed Koch, George Harvey, Joe Humphreys, and Charlie Meck to figure out their secrets and share the results with the rest of the world.

Though Pennsylvania is at the heart of spring creek country in the East, Virginia's Mossy Creek

Though the geologic factors that create the fertile waters of Western spring creeks are different than Eastern streams, the results are similar: selective trout rising to prolific hatches in clear water. DePuy's Spring Creek, near Livingston, Montana.
JOHN RANDOLPH PHOTO

Virginia's Mossy Creek is famous for its Sulphur hatches. Like many spring creeks, it flows through farm country.

provides anglers with the chance to cast to selective trout during immense Sulphur hatches just three hour's from the nation's capital. Outside of Hagerstown, Maryland, Beaver Creek provides winter angling to trout rising to midges because of its spring-fed waters. North of Pennsylvania, near Rochester, New York, anglers can fish the spring-fed Oatka and Spring Creeks.

Similar to the hallowed limestone spring creeks of Pennsylvania, and in similar farm country, are the

Spring Creeks	Freestone Streams
Limestone geology or volcanic	Sandstone and shale geology
High pH	Low pH
Low gradient, begin in valleys	High gradient, begin on mountains
Cold water through the summer	Warm water in the summer
Stable flows year-round	Fluctuating flows
Abundance (fish and insects)	Diversity (fish species and insects)

Stable flows, stable temperatures, and abundant food create prime growing conditions for spring creek trout. Because of the dense vegetation, even if you are skillful enough to hook one of the larger specimens, landing it is another matter.

spring creeks of the Midwest's three-corners region, where Minnesota, Iowa, and Wisconsin meet. In this region, better known as the Driftless Area, miles and miles of spring creeks offer fantastic fishing. Because of that region's limestone geology, the spring creeks resemble many of Pennsylvania's small spring creeks. Spring Branch (Iowa), South Branch of the Root River (southeast Minnesota), and West Fork of the Kickapoo River (Wisconsin) are a few of the miles of limestone creeks that flow in the Midwest. Many of these streams have not been publicized as much as the streams in Pennsylvania, yet they provide exceptional fishing.

Montana's aptly named Paradise Valley (near Livingston) is home to some beautiful spring creek streams, as well as many other streams that I hold dear to my heart. Many of these spring creeks twist and turn through grassy, wide-open ranges within the vast valleys. Eastern spring creek anglers will feel comfortable fishing DePuy's or Nelson's on their first time out West, though some of the larger rivers, such as the Henry's Fork or Missouri (a tailwater that fishes like a spring creek), might prove a challenge to anglers used to fishing smaller water. Mike Lawson, author of the definitive work on Western spring creeks (*Spring Creeks,* Stackpole Books), calls the Henry's Fork home, which is an enormous spring creek. I've read that Western spring creeks such as the Henry's Fork or Idaho's Silver Creek, California's Fall River, and Oregon's upper Metolious are volcanic, not limestone, in origin, but when I've fished some of the West's spring creeks, the results are more or less the same: cold, clean water, heavy hatches, and difficult trout.

So what makes a spring creek different than a freestone stream? Unlike most freestone streams, classic spring creeks or limestoners (see sidebar "What's in a Name?" on page 10) derive most of their flow from an underground source and are subsequently influenced by the region's geology; have high pH, consistent flow, and cold water; and typically have mild gradients. What follows is a

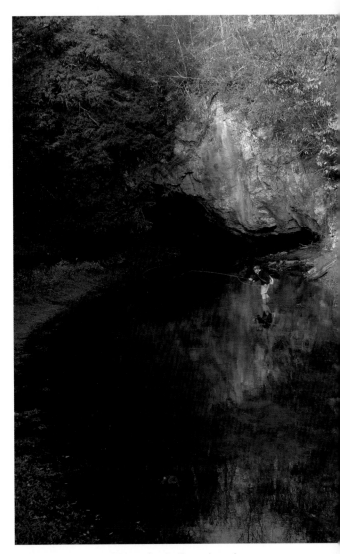

Sinking Run, in central Pennsylvania, flows through an enormous limestone arch (above). Arch Spring, the source of this part of Sinking Run, discharges from 2,000 to an estimated maximum of 30,000 gallons per minute. JACK HANRAHAN PHOTO

simplified explanation of some of these characteristics. For a more detailed explanation, I urge you to read Ted Leeson's fine book *Jerusalem Creek* (The Lyons Press), especially the chapter "Springs Eternal," which is a superb explanation of the geologic intricacies of spring creeks, among other

What's in a Name: Spring Creeks, Limestoners, Chalk Streams

As Ted Leeson points out in *Jerusalem Creek*, "spring creek" is more of a fishermen's word than a strict scientific classification, and the term oversimplifies a complex set of factors. But, as Leeson notes, "there is a rough logic" to our tradition of dividing streams up by their source of origin, such as freestone and spring creeks—or tailwaters if they flow from a dam. When I refer to spring creeks in this book, I am most often referring to the type of streams that are near and dear to me—the limestone-influenced creeks of Pennsylvania.

In my neck of the woods, spring creeks are also called "limestoners," but all limestoners are not pure spring creeks. According to Meck's broad definition of the word in *Fishing Limestone Streams*, a limestone stream can be any stream influenced enough by the region's geology (limestone, or calcium carbonate) to have high alkalinity. He breaks them down into four main categories, and in thinking about your local waters, you might begin to see how neat little classifications can become blurry. Meck breaks limestone streams down into "classic limestone streams" that emerge from a pool or spring such as the upper Letort or Falling Spring Branch (these are the streams that I fish and guide on most often); streams that begin as freestone streams have spring waters flowing into them, such as lower Bald Eagle Creek that is revitalized with Spring Creek's flows; freestone streams that have limestone springs along their lengths, which influence water temperature and pH; or freestone streams that begin in the mountains, but flow underground and reemerge as limestone streams. As Meck writes in *Fishing Limestone Streams*, "Many limestone streams exhibit a combination of one, two, or three of the types. Look at Spruce Creek in central Pennsylvania. Spruce Creek begins as a collection of several unnamed freestone streams that go underground. Then the limestone section of Spruce Creek erupts as a spring-fed pool near Rock Springs. Several miles downstream, just below Baileyville, dozens of additional springs enter the main stem."

Chalk stream is the word that people in the United Kingdom use to describe what Meck calls a "classic limestone stream." Chalk is a type of limestone (calcium carbonate) and, where the right geologic conditions exist, creates waterways that are very similar to limestone streams of southcentral Pennsylvania: an abundance of aquatic vegetations such as watercress, placid currents, high pH levels, and cool water. Famous chalk streams include the Test and Itchen, which are similar in character to some of the spring creeks in Pennsylvania.

There is another world of spring creeks that I am not nearly as intimate with, but nonetheless have fond memories of exploring: the waters of the American West. In addition to limestone or chalk geology, many springs are formed from volcanic activity and enriched by volcanic basalt. Leeson does an superb job of explaining the geology in *Jerusalem Creek*, and Mike Lawson's fantastic *Spring Creeks* goes into more detail about these types of streams. What all these streams have in common—the English chalk streams, the classic Pennsylvania limestoners, and Western waters such as the famed Henry's Fork—are cold water, great hatches, and fish that, as Mike Lawson puts best, you rarely catch by mistake.

things. Another great resource for understanding spring creeks, which are sometimes locally called "limestoners," is Charles Meck's *Fishing Limestone Streams* (The Lyons Press).

The Source

If we're painting with a broad brush, we can say that spring creeks "spring forth" from under the ground and freestone streams flow from water sources above ground such as rain and snowmelt. A spring is a definable location where groundwater naturally emerges from the earth, either in a pool or stream. Springs can discharge water onto the ground, forming a stream or part of a stream, or discharge water into the bed of an existing stream. The flow can be barely detectable, in which case it may be called a seep, or a gushing torrent, forming all or part of a trout stream. According to Charles Meck in *Fishing Limestone Streams,* "Pennsylvania has at least eleven springs that flow with more than 6,000 gallons per minute." Seeps and small springs can occur wherever the water table meets the land; large springs such as Big Spring or Boiling Springs Run typically form from water gushing up through fissures in the rock or flowing up through porous material. Both Big Spring and Boiling Springs have median flows over 11,000 gallons per minute.

The Water Cycle

The water for both freestone streams and spring creeks primarily comes from precipitation, though there are exceptions. Spring creeks draw on a larger reserve of water that has seeped far below the ground and has built up over a long period of time, whereas freestone streams derive their flow primarily from surface runoff. After it rains, water hits the earth, where it either runs off quickly or is absorbed into the soil. Water that is absorbed into the soil gets used up by a lot of things such as trees and plants, and the remaining water filters

down and becomes groundwater, eventually becoming stored in underlying aquifers. These aquifers are not underground wells or lakes, but water trapped in between grains of rock and sediment. Water in the soil doesn't move very far; groundwater can travel great distances, eventually

One skill to develop in spring creek fishing is learning how to present your fly in the lanes of clear water that flow through vegetation. At times, nymph fishing can be difficult, which may be why anglers often prefer dry-fly fishing.

discharging to surface water such as lakes and rivers or directly into the ocean.

Where groundwater has access to the land surface, you get a spring. Springs commonly occur in one of two ways. The most common is where the groundwater trickles down through porous earth and rock until it hits impermeable rock, moves along the top of that rock, and emerges as a spring. This frequently occurs on hillsides. In the case of many large gushing springs that form the headwaters of some of the famous spring creeks, cracks in the underground rock allow the groundwater to move from the aquifer to the surface.

Groundwater from a spring can issue onto the land surface or directly into a stream.

Because these streams bubble up from under the ground, geology plays a critical role in creating the perfect trout habitat that spring creeks are known for. In a nutshell, as the water passes through the rock (whether it is chalk in England, limestone in the Eastern United States, or volcanic basalt in the West) it not only increases in pH, but it also picks up important nutrients that create ideal nourishment for aquatic vegetation, fish, and the food fish eat (see sidebar "The pH Factor" on page 13).

Tailwaters, such as this section of the Yampa River below Stagecoach Reservoir in Colorado, are like man-made spring creeks. They have stable flows, cold water, and abundant hatches.

The pH Factor

Acidity or alkalinity is measured with a pH value. Water with a pH of less than 7 is considered acidic, and water with a pH greater than 7 is called basic, or alkaline. Water with a pH of 7 is considered "neutral." What does "pH" stand for? As far as I can tell, nobody knows for sure, but I have read that it might come from "potential of hydrogen," which points to the complex chemistry involved in either raising or lowering a pH value.

Generally speaking, water that is high in alkalinity can support more life than acidic water. Since most Eastern spring creeks flow through limestone geology, they have a high pH. Limestone is high in alkalinity and wherever spring creeks flow through it, like the creeks in southcentral Pennsylvania, they are enriched. Volcanic activity in a region (volcanic basalt) can also provide a similar effect on pH and provide the right geologic conditions for a spring creek, which is the case for many streams out West.

Limestone rock is composed largely of calcite or calcium carbonate. Calcium carbonate is Mother Nature's way of purifying the water. Many water treatment facilities use calcium carbonate, or "lime," to treat acidic water. Calcium carbonate also helps remove heavy metals in the water and adds nutrients. For anglers, a high pH most often means a healthier stream and heavier hatches, though many acidic freestone streams can also provide good fishing. Dense weed growth and aquatic vegetation is another sign of high pH, and these weeds house lots of insect nymphs and crustaceans. Freestone streams that have been polluted with acid from mines, acid rain, or other influences typically have lower pH values. Areas rich in limestone can mitigate the acidity of freestone streams.

A spring creek's cool flows, high pH (in Pennsylvania, most healthy spring creeks have pH levels around 8), and increased nutrients create ideal conditions for weed beds such as duckweed and elodea, which in turn provide cover for many different types of aquatic insects, baitfish, crayfish—and the trout that feed on them. When I am guiding new clients, I often grab a small clump of moss and shake it in my hand. With one shake, my hand is green with sow bugs, scuds, and *Baetis* nymphs, among other foods. Once new spring creek anglers observe how much food the fish have to eat, they understand why spring creek trout can afford to have fussy tastes, and why we may have to make many casts or change flies repeatedly to catch fish.

This dense vegetation provides a unique set of fishing challenges. The slow currents, meanders, and deep currents combined with weeds and grasses are both a blessing for their terrific trout habitat and a curse when you are trying to draw out a trout. Combine that with the clear water and fish that have everything they need, and you can have a tough time getting trout to take your fly.

In addition to the alkalinity and nutrients, the water is also cold. Summer water temperatures may fluctuate, depending on the number of springs and the size of the spring creek, but spring creeks remain cold and fishable all summer. Stream temperatures are usually around 53 degrees at the spring source. As the stream flows away from the source, the water warms up. Temperatures can range from 57 to the mid-60s as the water flows downstream.

During winter, spring creeks do not freeze. Though a spring creek may drop into the high 40s when snow is melting, average temperatures usually hover around 50 degrees. The stable temperatures provide year-round dry-fly fishing opportunities. On most winter days, you can expect

Part of the magic of fishing some Eastern spring creeks are the old buildings and sense of history. While charm doesn't catch you more fish, it definitely can add to the overall experience. JACK HANRAHAN PHOTO

A spring creek's stable water temperatures ensure year-round dry-fly fishing. JACK HANRAHAN PHOTO

to encounter trout rising to midges and late in fall and early spring, Blue-Winged Olives.

The stable flows also provide a dependable and relatively easy life for the stream's occupants. Unlike freestoners, which are subject to harsh scouring from runoff and exposed streambeds baking in the summer sun during drought years, spring creeks tend to keep a relatively steady water flow, allowing insect populations, vegetation, and trout to thrive. This stability provides a good flow of water when freestoners are unfishable and also provides clear water when other streams may be too muddy to fish.

Most spring creeks are clear, though some limestoners that rise up from softer geological formations have a chalky color. As the water rises, it brings with it fine particles that add color to the stream. The murkiness of the stream may vary, depending on how much flow is pouring out of the springs. More water can lead to more color, and less flow equals fewer particles. Water clarity can also be attributed to the stream's gradient. If the spring creek is much swifter, then more fine silt will be found in the current, leading to water with a tint, such as Penns Creek in central Pennsylvania.

Tailwater streams, such as the Bighorn, Rio Grande, and upper Delaware rivers, are entirely manmade, but they share striking resemblances to spring creeks in both character and the tactics required to be successful on them. Tailwaters are formed by large man-made reservoirs that release water from bottom-release systems. This water is icy cold and stays cold for miles downstream of the dam. Tailwaters are also full of nutrients and have good oxygen levels, which in turn lead to abundant insect life and dense vegetation. Like spring creeks, tailwaters are not usually affected by runoff from heavy rainfall and snowmelt and provide consistent year-round fishing because they have constant water flows and cool water temperature. Just as spring creeks teach you to become a better angler wherever you fish, many of the techniques you master on tailwaters work well on spring creeks.

CHAPTER 2

Because there are fewer species of insects in a spring creek than a freestone stream, a box stocked with different imitations for Baetis, Sulphurs or PMDs, and Tricos will serve most of your day-to-day mayfly needs.

JACK HANRAHAN PHOTO

Mayflies

Most spring creeks have outstanding hatches; they are sometimes so heavy that fishing can be tough. Because of the cold water, most spring creeks have relatively few species, which simplifies planning for the hatches. Each fishery is different, but I'll discuss the three major hatches you are likely to encounter on most spring creeks across the country: Blue-Winged Olives, Pale Morning Duns, and Tricos. Armed with knowledge of, and imitations for, these big three, you'll be way ahead of the game. These insects are also the most important on freestone and tailwater fisheries across the country. Though these three will provide a solid base for any angler's fly boxes, you can match your local mayfly hatches by changing the size and color of the different patterns provided here.

Blue-Winged Olives

Blue-Winged Olives (*Baetis*) are the first mayflies to hatch on many spring creeks across the country. *Baetis* live in most cold-water streams, from Idaho's Silver Creek to Big Spring in Newville, Pennsylvania, where they hatch just about every day of the year. *Baetis* love dreary, cold days, and I have fished over this hatch under the worst of conditions— when a cold drizzle has soaked me to the bones or when snow shared the sky with fluttering duns.

Generally speaking, prime *Baetis* time is from February through April and then again in the fall.

Baetis duns emerge early and late in the season on many spring creeks.

Some streams have longer hatches, and on several spring creeks that I know of, *Baetis* can hatch almost any day of the year. The heaviest activity usually occurs when the water temperatures reach the high 40s into the low 50s. At this time, nymphs emerge from 11:00 AM to 3:00 PM during the spring and from 10:00 AM to 1:00 PM during fall. The exact times can fluctuate, depending on the stream's geographical location, but if you plan on fishing the hatch during the warmest part of the day, you'll be off to a good start. Before Blue-Winged Olive nymphs hatch, the wing pads on the nymph's thorax darken, so it often makes sense to turn over rocks or seine the stream to inspect sample nymphs, focusing on areas with aquatic weeds or riffles where the nymphs like to live.

The slender Blue-Winged Olive nymphs are usually aggressive swimmers, but before emerging, they lose much of their energy, and a slow dead-drift retrieve duplicates the gentle struggle of the natural floating to the surface. Some, however, swim to the surface to emerge. In these instances, you might need a more aggressive retrieve. To match this, try twitching your nymph when you fish it dead-drift or even fishing the nymph with a downstream swing.

Standard *Baetis* imitations such as Pheasant Tails and olive Gold-Ribbed Hare's Ears do fine, but over the years I have developed a nymph pattern (Mike's Baetis Nymph) to imitate the natural's color and movement for difficult fish and clear water. The most common sizes that I use range from #16-18, though I fish #20s during the fall and larger #14s early on in the season. *Baetis* are almost always larger in the spring, getting progressively smaller through the year. You can add a black bead or flashback to this pattern as well.

M. H. Snowshoe Emerger (*Baetis*)

Hook:	#14-18 Orvis 1639 or other 1X short, 1X fine curved hook
Thread:	Olive 8/0
Tail:	Spooled olive Antron
Abdomen:	Olive Orvis Spectrablend Nymph dubbing
Thorax:	Olive Fine and Dry
Wing:	Fibers from natural snowshoe rabbit's foot
Head:	Olive Fine and Dry

Many times, trout feed more on emerging nymphs, which are easier to capture because they have trouble breaking the water's surface as they try to emerge. In these cases, I like a Snowshoe

Mike's *Baetis* Nymph

Hook:	#14-20 Orvis 1524 or other 1X heavy, 2X long nymph hook
Thread:	Brown 8/0
Tail:	Olive pheasant tail
Rib:	Fine silver wire
Abdomen:	Olive pheasant tail
Thorax:	70 percent squirrel dyed olive and 30 percent gray squirrel blended
Wing Case:	Gray goose quill
Head:	Tying thread

In the winter and early spring, it is common to see *Baetis* duns on the snow.

Emerger or an olive and brown emerger with a gray CDC (cul-de-canard) loopwing. The pattern sits low in the film and the CDC wing imitates the natural trying to escape its nymphal shuck. Another of my favorites for emergers and duns is a BWO Parachute, which rides low in the surface and effectively imitates either the drifting emerger or dun. It is also easy to see.

Many *Baetis* that emerge in colder weather don't make it to adulthood. The tiny nymphs rise through the water column and drift suspended just below the surface as they try to shed their nymphal shucks. On cold days, many cannot penetrate the surface. If they are successful and make it through the surface, then the *Baetis* duns must drift at the mercy of the currents until their wings are completely dry. In these cases, a dead drift is often the best presentation. On windy days, emerging duns often get trapped in their nymphal shucks. At these times, I first start fishing with a CDC emerger. If I get refusals, I nip the emerger off and tie on something different to imitate the trapped, half-hatched dun, such as a Quigley Cripple.

Because the water is most often clear, trout have a full view of the dun, especially when they are feeding in calm water. Though a hackled fly is useful under some conditions, a flush-floating fly such as a Comparadun or parachute-style pattern is usually more effective. A Sparkle Dun, which is a Comparadun with an Antron tail, sits low in the film, and the Antron can resemble the shed nymphal skin. Because you and the line's disturbance on the water is masked by the broken water, riffle-feeding trout can be easier to cast over and sometimes allow for a few extra casts, but those lying in the slick, glassy flats require much more patience. If one of these fish refuses your pattern, wait until the trout rises again before you make another cast.

Traditional BWO

Hook:	#14-18 Orvis 4641 (1X wide, 1X fine, big eye)
Thread:	Olive 8/0
Body:	Olive Fine and Dry
Hackle:	Dark dun hackle
Head:	Thread

Note: Orvis big-eye hooks make threading tippet through the eye of small hooks a lot easier. According to Orvis, #22 hooks have the same size eye as a conventional #16, with only a modest (4.5%) increased in weight.

BWO Comparadun

Hook:	#14-22 Orvis 4641 (1X wide, 1X fine, big eye)
Thread:	Olive 8/0
Tail:	Olive Antron
Body:	Olive Fine and Dry
Wing:	Dark deer hair

Picking the Right Pattern

For many, dry-fly fishing is the essence of spring creek fishing, and it is without a doubt exhilarating. But matching what fish are eating on the surface is only part of the game. You need to be able to match what they are feeding on under the surface, which, because of the abundance of food down there, is where they often get their meals.

Trout eat lots of different foods. Mayflies, caddisflies, midges, and stoneflies are the aquatic insects that account for the bulk of a trout's diet. Many feel it is important to know every little thing about these bugs, but I think it is most important to just be able to distinguish one insect from the next and know when these insects hatch.

Pick up a few rocks, dig through weeds, or pull up a stick in a healthy spring creek and you will find a handful of insects. Besides cress bugs and shrimp (which we will talk about later), you might find mayfly and stonefly nymphs and caddis and midge larvae. Sounds like a scary mess, but it is not. Midge larvae are small and wormlike, with distinct heads and no legs. They come in a wide range of colors, with red, cream, black, and olive the most common. Caddis larvae look like small worms with three pairs of legs just below their heads and have three forms: Free-living caddis crawl on rocks and weeds without any case, purse-case makers look like free-living caddis larvae but build meshlike nets over themselves that help collect food, and case makers build houses of stones or sticks around themselves.

Stonefly nymphs are easy to distinguish from mayfly nymphs or caddis larvae if you remember that all their key features come in pairs. The stonefly nymph has two distinct thick tails and two antennae protruding from its head. The abdomen is slender with two wing cases of equal length in the thorax region. Mayfly nymphs, however, have only one set of wing pads and they do not have antennae. Depending on the exact species, mayfly nymphs have either two or three tails (*Baetis* have two long, slender tails; *Ephemerella* have three short, stout tails). All mayfly nymphs have six legs and an abdomen, thorax, and head.

The winged versions of the underwater insects are easier to identify. Adult mayflies (whether duns or spinners), also called upwings, hold their wings at a 90-degree angle from their bodies; caddisflies, also called tentwings, hold their wings tentlike over

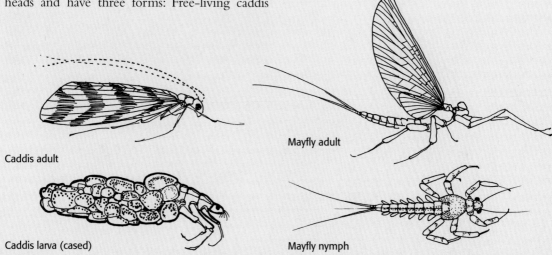

Caddis adult

Mayfly adult

Caddis larva (cased)

Mayfly nymph

their entire bodies; stoneflies, also called flatwings or downwings, hold their wings flat over their bodies. Midges are sometimes called flatwings and also glasswings. Midges also have puffy antennae atop their little heads. Except for a few midge species like craneflies or mosquitoes, these flies are tiny.

All mayflies, caddisflies, midges, and stoneflies have the same features from one stream to the next. Midges and caddisflies have a complete life cycle of egg, larva, pupa, and adult. Stoneflies and mayflies have an incomplete life cycle—they don't have a pupal stage. This becomes important to know down the road when you have to choose imitations to match the different stages.

In addition to being able to identify the various important trout stream insects, you should train yourself to pay careful attention to the insects' behaviors before, during, and after hatching, which directly correlates to fly pattern design and choice and, more importantly, how you fish those patterns.

Picking the right fly pattern doesn't have to always be a guessing game. Study nature's clues to narrow down the selection. JACK HANRAHAN PHOTO

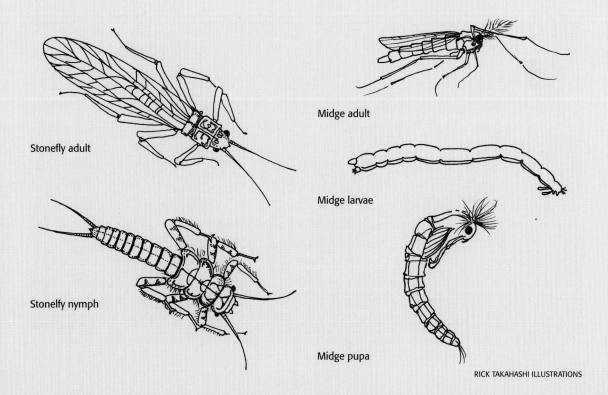

Stonefly adult

Stonelfy nymph

Midge adult

Midge larvae

Midge pupa

RICK TAKAHASHI ILLUSTRATIONS

In certain situations, a hackled pattern (traditional or thorax tie) is more effective than a low-riding parachute. The hackled pattern allows the flies to skate higher on the water's surface, which can be effective on a windy day. And yes, Blue-Winged Olives do hatch on windy days. If a dead-drift presentation is not working, walk or wade into position upstream of the rising trout and try skating your pattern across the surface just above the trout to imitate a dun being blown across the water's surface. If casting upstream, twitch the pattern as it reaches the feeding trout. You'll need patience and practice to master this technique, but make sure you start with a long leader and a well-dressed, hackled pattern.

After the male spinners gather above the stream, the females enter the swarm and begin mating. After mating, the females head to bankside vegetation to rest while their eggs develop. *Baetis* spinners crawl down anything that is protruding out of the water or dive into the water to deposit their eggs on vegetation, rocks, or wood debris under the water's surface. The spinners prefer to lay eggs in less turbulent water. This manner of egg-laying sets *Baetis* apart from other mayflies.

When they enter the water, their wings are folded back over their frail bodies, trapping air bubbles underneath the glassy wings. After depositing their eggs, the drowned female spinners helplessly drift with the water's current. Some float to the surface and drift like true spent spinners, while others drift subsurface. Often a traditional spent spinner imitation is not as effective during Blue-Winged Olive spinnerfalls as it is with other insects. But if there are enough floating female spinners, I have noticed trout feeding along the edges of the bank. A #18-20 BWO Parachute or olive Hackle Spinner has worked for me in these cases.

The best-case scenario is to fish wet flies dead drift in or below the water's film through where the trout are feeding. I first started fishing classic wet flies like the Leadwing Coachman and Blue

A flush-floating Comparadun can imitate the dun or the spinner and is an excellent choice for placid currents. JACK HANRAHAN PHOTO

Soft-Hackles

The soft-hackle is a style of tying more than a specific pattern. The body or abdomen is tied sparse, and a small ball of fur is wrapped just before the head. Then a wrap or two of partridge or other soft feather is used to form the collar, which pulses seductively as the fly drifts. Some fly fishermen have forgotten about soft-hackles, but this time-tested pattern's long history in the fly boxes of successful anglers testifies to its effectiveness.

I love using soft-hackles for mimicking certain insects like BWO spinners and diving caddis, but also use them to imitate mayflies by varying the body color and ribbing material. While I most often use hen or partridge, you can also use grouse, starling, and many other feathers.

BWO Soft-Hackle

Hook:	#14-20 Orvis 1639 or other 1X short, 1X fine curved hook
Thread:	To match body
Abdomen:	Floss, fine wire, or dubbing to match insect color
Thorax:	Fur dubbing
Legs:	Hen saddle or Hungarian partridge

Dun, but over the years I have found that olive soft-hackles performed better during spinnerfalls. I tie a simple soft-hackle pattern to imitate the drowned female spinner with light olive synthetic dubbing and a turn or two of Hungarian partridge just before the hook eye. Once submerged in the water, the partridge folds back over the body, just as the natural spinner folds back her wings, and the synthetic dubbing holds tiny air bubbles. The partridge also pulsates, mimicking the female's gentle struggle to release her eggs.

Eastern Sulphurs

Sulphurs are probably the most anticipated mayfly hatches of the entire season. Eastern hatches are referred to as Sulphurs (*Ephemerella* sp.), while in the Midwest and West insects of the same genus are re-ferred to as Pale Morning Duns. Sulphur hatches can last for a month or more once they get started. On southern Pennsylvania spring creeks, Sulphur hatches begin in mid-May and finish by late June. On some Eastern spring creeks, Sulphurs hatch into July.

Sulphur nymphs prefer moderately fast riffles and crawl around on weeds, rocks, and other sunken debris. They are poor swimmers, so when dislodged, they drift helplessly in the current until they regain their hold on the stream bottom or vegetation. Before hatching, the nymphs migrate to slower currents, where they wait until the time is right to emerge. The nymphs can be swept away from their cover and drift in the currents at any time of the year, but this occurs most frequently just before a hatch, when the nymphs start to move more. To emerge, the nymphs swim to just below

Sulphurs (named for the orangish-yellow body color) are the Eastern equivalent to Western Pale Morning Duns (PMDs). These yellow bugs are the most important and consistent hatch on spring creeks in the late spring and summer.

the water's surface. The nymphs make several attempts to break through the surface film, and once they have done so, they shed their nymphal shucks and officially become duns. Like *Baetis* nymphs, Sulphur nymphs' wing cases begin to darken about a week or so before they hatch.

A #14-18 dark brown nymph works well on most streams where Sulphurs live, which is probably why the Pheasant Tail is such a popular all-purpose nymph pattern. Fish a Sulphur nymph imitation dead drift along the bottom by casting upstream or across the stream and allowing the fly to sink and drift naturally. On small streams, I usually fish the nymphs on a tight line, adjusting split shot so the fly drifts close to and ticks bottom every now and then. If I catch bottom too much, I remove some shot.

There are three main species of Sulphurs. The two larger Sulphurs, *Ephemerella invaria* and *E. rotunda* (#14-16), are yellow with noticeable hints of olive. They begin to hatch first, before the smaller Sulphur. The larger two Sulphurs usually hatch during the early evening. On cooler, cloudier days, they can hatch from 11:00 AM throughout the afternoon. Warmer weather often delays the hatch to later in the evening—7:00 PM to dusk. The

smaller Sulphur, *E. dorothea* (#16-18), generally has a pale yellow body, begins to hatch about two weeks after the larger Sulphurs appear on the water, and hatches later in the evening. Like all aquatic insects, a Sulphur's body color can vary from stream to stream or region to region. The *invaria* and *rotunda* Sulphurs range from pale yellow to yellow, with a light-olive cast through their bodies. The smaller *dorothea* Sulphurs can be pale to bright yellow and have orange thoraxes, a trait the Shenk Sulphur Dun and other popular patterns capitalize on.

As more Sulphur nymphs hatch, a fair number drift just below the surface. Trout that you observe surface-feeding without taking the duns or not fully breaking the surface are most likely feeding on emerging nymphs. If you do not see bubbles on the surface of the water after a fish has risen, then chances are it has actually taken a fly from under the surface. To effectively imitate emerging nymphs, try fishing floating nymph patterns or emerging nymph imitations dead drift.

Even though you fish these patterns on a dead drift, tie or buy flies with materials that move in the water. Movement can be built into the fly by using CDC or dubbing with a blend of Antron. The Antron adds a little shimmer to fur bodies. My M. H. Snowshoe Emerger is an emerging nymph tied on a bent hook. The abdomen is brown dubbing to match the back of the nymph, and the yellow thorax simulates the partially freed dun emerging from the nymphal shuck. The wing is snowshoe rabbit's foot. The CDC and the snowshoe rabbit hair float in the film, and the rest hangs below the surface. On the water, these two materials mimic the gentle struggle of the emerging nymph.

After the male duns hatch, they quickly molt and change into yellowish brown spinners. As more and more male and female duns hatch, male spinners congregate over the riffles to wait for the females to fly into the swarms to mate. After mating, male spinners seldom fall to the water. I have spent many nights looking for spent spinners only

Mike's Sulphur and *Baetis* Nymph

I designed my Sulphur and *Baetis* nymphs back in 1985. I was having difficulties catching trout with the patterns I was using. At the time, I didn't know if it was my lack of skill or simply the wrong fly. I had the basic idea of how to tie dry flies, nymphs, and streamers, but certainly not enough money to purchase any of the great books on insects and patterns. I did have Caucci and Nastasi's *Instant Mayfly Identification Guide,* which helped me identify several insects in my area. It was handy to carry because it is a thin, plastic-bound booklet. So one day, I put my rod aside and collected a few Sulphur nymphs. I figured if I had a few to see, I could pattern a fly from the live insect.

Immediately, I noticed several dissimilarities when I compared the patterns I was using to the live insects. My Sulphur pattern was lighter than the live specimen. My fly patterns were also too big and had little, if any, natural movement. I then took a closer look at the live insect, picking out all the key features that could possibly make that perfect fly: a short, stubby tail about half the body length; an abdomen darker than the thorax; and a dark wingcase to imitate the natural ready to emerge. The same went for the *Baetis* nymph. I was using a pattern that did not match the fly as effectively as I thought it should have. In clear water, spring creek trout get as good a look at a nymph as they do a surface dry fly.

I began working on designing these two fly patterns. Through trial and error, I found suitable materials to effectively match both the Sulphur and *Baetis* nymphs. The Sulphur was mottled brown, with a stout tail and fat body. The *Baetis* nymph had a slender, two-toned body; a long, thin tail; and a dark wing case. My fly patterns looked good to me, but the true test would be how trout responded to them.

It did not take long before I found that trout liked these two flies. For years, I fished my Sulphur nymph on Falling Spring and caught trout after trout. Not all that long ago, a good friend, John Williams, invited me to fish the Little Lehigh on a chilly, drizzly spring day. We could see trout feeding in the clear water, but they were tough to fool. Finally, John landed one, and hoping to find out what it was feeding on, I pumped its stomach and discovered it was eating Blue-Winged Olive nymphs. I gave John my *Baetis* nymph and tied one on myself, and we both caught fish after fish on that fly. My Sulphur and *Baetis* nymphs have worked well for me all over the country.

Mike's Sulphur Nymph

Hook:	#14-18 Orvis 1524 or other 1X heavy, 2X long nymph hook
Thread:	Brown 8/0
Tail:	Grouse back feather or brown hen back feather
Rib:	Fine gold wire
Abdomen:	70 percent fox squirrel and 30 percent Awesome Possum blended
Thorax:	Same as abdomen
Wing Case:	Wild turkey tail
Head:	Tying thread

to find more hatching duns. The female spinners fly back to the bank, where they wait for the egg sacs to develop. Then the females drop or dip their fully developed egg sacs into the water. Some may not fall to the water as spent spinners. However, *E. dorothea* spinners do fall to the water and lie spent. Many times anglers mistake this small Sulphur for one of the larger species.

Spinnerfalls start as the duns continue to hatch. The exact time of a spinnerfall depends greatly on air temperatures. On cool evenings, the spinners begin to gather over the riffles earlier in the evening, about 5:00 PM. If the night air temperature is in the mid-70s into the 80s, spinners often wait until dusk. On these nights I find a comfortable place to sit until the spinners begin dancing over the water. On hot and humid evenings, Sulphurs sometimes begin their mating flights just as the sun sets, and they continue into nightfall. I can remember several occasions fishing to trout rising to Sulphurs well past 10:00 PM during these conditions.

Trout become finicky during Sulphur hatches and spinnerfalls, especially if they unfold during daylight hours. Hatching duns float on the water's surface for long periods, and a dead drift is the best way to present your fly. If you are down or across-stream of the rising fish, gently cast your fly no farther than twelve inches from and just to one side of the trout. Try to hit a target the size of a twelve-inch pie plate just at the fish's nose. If you cast too far upstream, the fly may drag before it reaches the fish. Keep the cast gentle. You do not want the fly line to splash on the water. A traditional hackled fly works when you are fishing more turbulent areas in the stream, but in calmer waters, a Comparadun or thorax tie works best.

At night, duns and spinners are usually on the water simultaneously. Because Sulphurs hatch for a long period of time, other insects, including egg-laying caddis, may be on the water. Emerging Sulphur duns, Sulphur spinners, and egg-laying caddis all float low on the surface. Many times the trout become less sensitive to color and focus more on

the pattern's silhouette. One hot evening, I was patiently waiting for the first Sulphurs to appear in Fox's Meadow on Letort Spring Run. The water was cool, the air was hot and humid, and the mixture made a lazy haze over the stream. About 6:00 PM, Sulphurs began to flutter into the evening light and a few small trout began to break through the glassy surface. With a pale yellow #16 Comparadun, I took a small brown.

About 8:30 PM, the hatch was in full gear, and at a gentle bend in the stream, which was protected by overhanging trees and bushes, I heard a loud splash. I worked my way upstream, and the brown broke the surface once again. Changing fly patterns several times, I spent one hour patiently working this trout. At dusk, I could not see my flies, but the brown continued to rise, and I kept casting. By 9:15, I was as blind as a bat and thought the trout would be looking for low-floating flies. I tied on a parachute, and two casts later I heard a gulp where I thought my fly might be. I lifted my rod and felt the line tighten. It was a trout or a tree. Patience had paid off, and I brought to hand a nice eighteen-inch brown trout.

At dark, I like a pattern that has more surface contact and imitates several insects at once. A fly that can multitask makes life much easier when there are multiple insects hatching at once and changing flies is difficult because it's hard to see the hook eye. When Sulphurs and caddis are on the water together, I usually start fishing a Hi-Vis Parachute Sulphur. I can easily see the fluorescent-orange post, and the fly floats low on the surface, providing a plausible imitation of any insect riding in the film.

Western Pale Morning Duns

Pale Morning Duns or PMDs (*Ephemerella infrequens* and *E. inermis*) are the Western versions of Eastern Sulphurs. PMDs are widely dispersed through the Midwest into California and are important hatches on most streams they inhabit.

They thrive in weed-choked spring creeks and tailwaters but can be found throughout the Rocky Mountains.

Once underway, PMD hatches can last for several months, along with many other types of hatching insects. The exact start of PMD hatches can be hard to predict because the mayfly inhabits many different streams and is so widely dispersed. Stream conditions such as water type, runoff, and temperature affect the timing of the hatch. In general, Pale Morning Duns can be on the water as early as May and then last into October. Cool spring runoff usually delays the hatch; streams in California with warmer water flows, the spring creeks of Iowa, and streams influenced by warm spring water, such as those in Yellowstone, can have early hatches of PMDs. For instance, on the Fall River, California's largest spring creek, blizzard PMD spinnerfalls can begin in late May and last into June, occurring from midmorning to early afternoon. On the Henry's Fork, Pale Morning Duns (*Ephemerella inermis*) emerge in midmorning

Pale Morning Duns or PMDs (*Ephemerella infrequens* and *E. inermis*) thrive in weed-choked spring creeks such as Dana Spring Creek (above) and tailwaters. JOHN RANDOLPH PHOTO

Snowshoe Emergers

Like most February days on the Yellow Breeches, several trout were rising. I quickly tied on a small midge to 7X tippet and began casting. Try as I might, I did not fare well. On closer inspection, I realized that what I thought were midges actually was a light Blue-Winged Olive hatch.

After kicking myself for not looking more closely to begin with, I tied on a Blue-Winged Olive (BWO) pattern, but I still had refusal after refusal. Feeling a little beat up, I just watched, trying to learn something. I noticed that, because of the cold air temperatures, the BWOs could not get free from the water's surface and were just drifting in the surface film. I had no pattern that would ride that low.

I went home puzzled, but I soon found inspiration from some snowshoe rabbit's foot fur that I had bought at a fly-fishing show. Fur from the rabbit's foot has natural oils in it that repel water and help the hare keep warm during winter. With a hot cup of coffee, I started thinking of how to get a fly to sit lower in the water. After several attempts, a fly was beginning to come to life from between the jaws of my vise. When I saw how effective this pattern was for *Baetis,* I developed color variations to match Sulphurs and Tricos. I also modified the sizes and colors to match other mayfly emergers, including Hendricksons and March Browns.

If you fish these patterns, or any other snowshoe flies, do not use liquid floatant with snowshoe rabbit because it mattes the fibers and compromises its flotation properties. I apply a powder floatant to the snowshoe fibers with a brush. For a photo and recipe for the Baetis M.H. Snowshoe Emerger, see page 18; for a photo and recipe of the Trico M. H. Snowshoe Emerger, see page 34.

M. H. Snowshoe Emerger (Sulphur)

Hook:	#14-18 Orvis 1639 or other 1X short, 1X fine curved hook
Thread:	Yellow 8/0
Tail:	Cream Antron
Abdomen:	Brown Orvis Spectrablend Nymph dubbing
Thorax:	Yellow Fine and Dry
Wing:	Fibers from a snowshoe rabbit's foot
Head:	Yellow Fine and Dry

and there are spinnerfalls both at dusk and in the morning from mid June through early July.

PMD nymphs can be fished just like their Eastern counterparts—dead-drift and as close to the bottom as possible. They are most effective before and during a hatch, but #14-16 brownish red nymphs can be bottom-bounced year-round. PMD nymphs migrate to slower waters before they hatch, and during the hatch, they make several attempts to emerge as duns. At this point, I like to fish CDC or Snowshoe Emergers dead drift in the surface film. Floating nymphs fished in the same way can also be effective, especially if you twitch them softly to mimic the struggling insect while it drifts in the surface film. When strong winds, riffled water, and cool weather prevent duns from hatching, crippled or stillborn imitations fit the bill.

PMDs that successfully escape their nymphal shucks spend a long time in the drift, especially on cool days. PMD duns (#16-18) are yellow with a distinct olive cast and pale gray wings with a hint of pale yellow on the leading edge. I like to fish Comparaduns and parachutes that match the color and size of the naturals if I notice trout breaking the surface to take drifting duns. Sometimes PMD duns try to escape the water's surface quickly during warm weather. In that case, wise trout may be looking for a pattern that rides higher on the water. Hackled imitations may work better then because less of the fly's profile is on the water and the suggestion of movement becomes more important.

Pale Morning Dun spinnerfalls unfold just like their eastern counterparts, except PMDs fall to the water as spent spinners. Duns molt into spinners and then gather above the riffles to mate. Females drop their egg sacs into the water, and then both male and female fall spent to the water's surface. Weather decides when all this takes place. Typically, spinners hover above the water later in the evening into dusk, but hot weather may delay spinnerfall until the next morning. The midmorning spinnerfall on Fall River is one of the premier events in fly fishing.

Spring Creek (near State College, Pennsylvania) has fantastic Sulphur hatches in the evening, but as the hatch continues through summer, the fish become more selective.

Mike Lawson and Ed Engle figure the spinner-fall to be the best time to take full advantage of this hatch, and according to Rene Harrop in his excellent *Fly Fisherman* article, "Pondering PMDs," "If there is a time when fishing PMDs can be simplified, it is during a spinnerfall. This is not to imply that it will be easy, but certainly there are fewer variables to contend with when trout lock into the spent-wing phase."

PMD spinners float low in the water's film, fully spent, which is inviting to the trout. Rusty Spinners with Antron, McFlylon, Krystal Flash, or clipped hackle wings and dubbed or biot bodies are popular patterns and work well for spinners across the country. Though PMD spinnerfalls vary in color from region to region, spinner patterns in olive-yellow or rusty brown fished with a drag-free presentation fool most trout. Flush-floating patterns become hard to see during low light, and it may make sense to fish your spinner behind an easy-to-see dry fly or fish a parachute pattern with a highly visible wing post.

Shenk Sulphur Dun

Hook:	#14-18 Orvis 4641 (1X wide, 1X fine, big eye)
Thread:	Yellow 8/0
Abdomen:	Pale yellow Fine and Dry
Thorax:	Sulphur yellow Fine and Dry
Hackle:	Cream or white hackle
Head:	Tying thread

Note: The Shenk Sulphur Dun works great at any time during the hatch, and it made me realize I did not have to include a wing on my fly patterns. They catch fish on the Letort, so they are winners in my book.

Hi-Vis Sulphur Parachute

Hook:	#14-18 Orvis 4641 (1X wide, 1X fine, big eye)
Thread:	Yellow 8/0
Body:	Pale yellow Fine and Dry
Post:	Fluorescent-orange-dyed turkey flats
Hackle:	Cream or white hackle

Note: The Hi-Vis Parachute is easy to see in low light. It floats low and can be mistaken for other insects that may be on the water come dark.

Tricos

As the final days of June slip into July, many fly fishers mourn the passing of the fat hatches of spring. I don't. I'm excited because my best days of the trout season are still ahead. All year I look forward to sultry July mornings with the sun burning orange through the heavy, humid air as it rises over a watercress meadow. Trico time is my time.

My favorite description of the Trico phenomenon came from the late Vincent Marinaro in an article he wrote for *Outdoor Life* back in 1969. Marinaro, a corporate tax lawyer by profession and a highly original designer of trout flies by avocation, spent the happiest days of his life stalking his beloved limestone streams. He described the emergence and death dance of *Tricorythodes* mayflies—and their delirious effect on trout—as the "white curse." If there's a more perfect description of such a captivating, demanding hatch, I haven't heard it.

I vividly recall the first time I saw them. On a July morning here in the green farm country of southcentral Pennsylvania, I had driven from my home in Fayetteville over to Chambersburg to fish Falling Spring. I had fished this well-known stream several times before, and I had heard about Tricos, but I'd never actually seen any. The air was still. As the bright sun burst across the meadow, there they were: the bright wings of hundreds—thousands—of miniature mayflies, rising in glittering swarms from the gunmetal sheen of the water

to the dark, silhouetted branches overhead. As far as I could see, around every narrow bend, the airborne insects dipped and danced in elegant, transparent clouds. It was a breathtaking performance.

At first, not a single trout was visible. That quickly changed when the Tricos began hitting the water. Within minutes, rise after rise filled the placid run I was working. Glancing up and down the stream, I was almost overwhelmed by the seemingly endless number of rising trout. Standing there, you, too, would have thought it would be easy pickings. No! Although the trout were gulping down spent Trico after spent Trico, which seemed

Mating Tricos form dense clouds over the water on hot summer mornings. Charlie Meck (above) casts to risers on Spruce Creek.

In the East, hot hazy mornings with the sun burning through the clouds signals Trico time.

at the time to be no larger than the tip of a lead pencil, they were also the most finicky, pattern-selective, leader-shy trout I had ever encountered.

As frustrating as that experience was, my early failure made me determined to spend as much time as possible on the water during Trico time and learn everything I could about catching trout during these summer-morning feeding sprees. In the many seasons since, I've learned a thing or two about how to succeed when the trout turn their attention to Marinaro's famous white curse.

They are the most reliable summertime hatches on trout streams throughout the country, and your favorite stream may just have a good hatch. In the West, the principal species is *Tricorythodes minutus*; in the East, it's the slightly smaller *Tricorythodes stygiatus*. Because these aquatic insects are so small and delicate, populations are most abundant in streams with moderate flows and fine bottoms. Tricos inhabit tailwater rivers, freestone streams, and cool-flowing spring creeks. Especially noted for prolific emergences are the Bighorn and Missouri rivers in Montana, the Au Sable River in Michigan, and the weed-choked eastern spring creeks such as Virginia's Mossy Creek and Pennsylvania's Falling Spring Branch, Little Lehigh, and legendary Letort Spring Run.

Tricos appear on some southern trout waters as early as the middle of May. On my home streams in Pennsylvania, Trico hatches begin in late June and continue through November. In the Midwest and into the West, they appear from July into late fall and sometimes well into November on some of the famous Paradise Valley spring creeks. I've heard some anglers say that the first killing frost ends Trico hatches. Not entirely. Although hatches diminish after the first frost, they are still around, and enough duns and spinners are often present to entice a trout or two to the surface.

Male dun imitations are usually dressed with black or dark brown bodies; female duns are tied with olive abdomens and dark brown thoraxes. Sizes vary from region to region. Imitations tied to represent just the single Trico are tied on a size 20 to 24 hook in the East and size 18 to 24 in the West. Popular Trico floaters are the standard hackle design, deer hair or CDC Comparaduns, and thorax ties.

Another effective fly is the Cluster Dun. During heavy hatches, duns cling together. Try two duns tied on one hook, which makes them easier to spot on the water. Double Trico patterns can be tied on hook sizes 16 through 20. Although both spinners are approximately the same size, the body of the male is entirely black, and the female features a white abdomen with a dark brown to blackish thorax.

Trout go crazy when these tiny mayflies hit the water. Some remarkably large fish move from their protective shelters and position themselves in plain sight, just below the surface, to dine on the parade of dark-bodied flies. Although normally calm pools are now erupting with energetically rising trout, these fish are not easy to catch. Stop everything and watch. You'll notice that many fish are rising routinely, some every few seconds. Get a feel for the rhythm of your target fish, and then time your cast and the anticipated drift of your fly precisely with the next time you expect the fish to rise.

Female Trico duns (above) have olive abdomens; males have black or dark-brown bodies.

M. H. Snowshoe Emerger (Trico)

Hook:	#18-22 Orvis 1639 or other 1X short, 1X fine curved hook
Thread:	Black 8/0
Tail:	Black Antron
Abdomen:	Black Orvis Spectrablend Nymph dubbing
Thorax:	Black Fine and Dry
Wing:	Fibers from a snowshoe rabbit's foot
Head:	Black Fine and Dry

Feeding trout may be taking emergers, duns, or spinners; only the keen eye of a patient angler will discern which. The common "head-and-tail" rise-form usually means the trout are taking duns and spinners. Sometimes just the nose of the trout breaks the water's surface; emergers are taken just below or low in the water's surface. For the most part, trout won't break the surface when feeding on emergers. Often these riseforms are just slight dimples on the surface. Trout keying on a particular stage commonly become spooky and extremely selective because their close station to the surface makes them vulnerable to birds and animals.

A trout feeding on Tricos moves only inches to sip the next morsel—or your fly. Imagine your window of opportunity as a ten-inch pie plate immediately upstream from a rising trout. Your fly has to land within that window and fall as gently

as dandelion fluff. A delicate cast that's right on target is vital. Your leader must be at least eleven feet and finished with 6X to 8X tippet.

True, the effectiveness of a nymphal imitation pales in comparison with dry-fly versions of duns and spinners, but trout can be taken with properly fished nymph patterns. Trico nymphs cling to submerged vegetation and crawl around the fine gravel. In larger rivers, the nymphs thrive both in slower edges and in the silt alongside faster currents. On the Bighorn, where I learned to fish a two-fly rig, a #18 Pheasant Tail with a #18-24 pale brown Trico nymph behind it was effective. Like my BWO and Sulphur nymphs, I also tie the Trico nymph with a darkened wingcase.

Trico nymphs are feeble swimmers, so when they are dislodged, a noticeable struggle isn't likely. The ideal way to present your nymph to the trout is with a dead drift. Fish your fly close to the bottom. Add or take off split shot until the drift is right. Takes are usually light when you fish these tiny nymphs. A small strike indicator can be a valuable asset for picking up such minute inhalations. On smaller streams or on shallow riffles in larger rivers, I like to fish Trico nymphs with the high-stick method. This technique keeps most of the line off the water, making it easier to detect strikes. A leader tapered to 4X is adequate on larger rivers or unpressured trout, but 5X is generally necessary on spring creeks.

Trout sometimes key on nymphs during a heavy hatch. Particularly wary fish abstain from eating duns and spinners and instead feed on the emerging flies. Many anglers fail to see this and assume a trout bulging on the surface is rising to duns or spinners. Again, takes are exceptionally light. A Trico nymph fished in or below the surface can be just the ticket. Another good fly to try is a CDC emerger with an olive-brown body and a loop of gray CDC to imitate the wings breaking through the nymphal shuck. You can dead drift a nymph in the water column, a foot or more deep, or just below the surface.

I don't like strike indicators when fishing emergers. Instead, I use the simple two-fly system. Tie a dry fly to the end of your tippet. (I normally use a Trico dun, but if you are unable to see a small fly, go with something bigger. A large terrestrial such as a cricket may suit you better.) Attach a ten- to twelve-inch piece of tippet material at the bend of the dry fly, and then tie the nymph or emerger to the end. If the dry "indicator fly" pauses or goes under during the drift, set the hook. I normally use 7X for the dropper and a clinch knot for both knots.

During the heat of the summer, prime Trico time, male Tricos emerge from the water first, often beginning just after sunset and continuing through the night. The females hatch the following morning beginning at daybreak. This is an important bit of intelligence, because when you get to the water and start stripping line off your reel first thing in the morning, few male duns may be on the surface; they'll already be up in the trees, molting. An imitation of a female dun is your best offering. I have often fished over good hatches of female Tricos during the early morning hours. On Montana's Bighorn River, the trout eagerly await the oncoming morning Trico hatch. The female duns hatch in incredible numbers. The opaque wings look smoky in color as the rising sun penetrates through the countless drifting female duns. A small, olive-bodied parachute or a simple hackle dry fly was a welcome pattern if drifted drag free over feeding trout. As the summer fades into fall, the evenings and mornings become cooler, and the emergence of male duns is typically delayed to just before sunrise, followed directly by the female duns. In these circumstances, both males and females are on the

When Trico spinners hit the water, trout feed steadily. Timing their rhythm is the key to success.

water at the same time, and once again olive-bodied dun patterns become effective until both male and female Tricos molt into spinners.

When the female duns begin to emerge, the male spinners begin to swarm high over the riffles and along the banks on larger waters. Sometime during the morning, the female duns molt into spinners. Air temperature determines when this happens. Warmer air temperatures mean an earlier molt; cooler temperatures mean a later molt. So the female duns may molt within minutes or hours after hatching. After molting, female spinners fly into the swarms, where the males grasp them to mate. After mating, the male spinners immediately fall to the water, where they are eaten by waiting trout. The female spinners make for

Check cobwebs near the stream for signs of a Trico hatch.

vegetation to wait for their egg sacs to develop, head back to the water to lay their eggs, and finally drift spent on their watery graves.

Generally speaking, the first of the male spinners fill the air by 7:00 AM. By 8:30 AM, the first spinners begin falling to the water. A heavy spinnerfall usually lasts several hours. The trout are highly attuned to this sequence. Watch how their behavior changes as the morning progresses. After two or three Trico mornings, you should pick up on their transition from feeding on duns to feeding on spinners. If you're unable to detect a change, look closely at the water and see if duns or spinners are drifting downstream. At first, a few trout switch their attention, and then nearly all will be feeding on spinners. Remember that the males fall to the water first. During the early stages of the spinnerfall, trout take male spinners exclusively, making the male spinner imitation your best bet. Before the female spinners fall to the water, they fly back and forth above the stream, an indication for you to be ready with female spinner imitations. If you don't notice the female flights, look to the water to determine what is drifting on the currents.

Most trout are completely engrossed when feeding on these minute but abundant morning concentrations of duns and spent spinners. Wise trout often let their guard down and forget about what lurks around them. So as trout begin to focus on the feeble duns and spinners, try narrowing the gap between you and the trout. Slowly creep into a position that is less than twenty feet away. Decreasing the distance between your rod tip and your fly helps eliminate fly drag. Depending on your eyesight, you just may be able to see the tiny Trico imitation. If you are unable to see the Trico, try a two-fly combo with a foam beetle or caddis attached to your tippet and a Trico attached to 14 inches of 6X or 7X.

Your best approach is from behind for several reasons. The fish is less likely to see you and your cast is in the same current as the feeding trout, which helps eliminate the dreaded drag. Many

When fishing to trout rising to Tricos, you often need to make long casts and use light tippets.

times a trout spooks to protective cover upon the appearance of something not natural or a threat—meaning a fly fisherman. In my experience, approaching a rising trout from the side is a last resort, but in the case of Tricos, it often becomes effective. Trico-sipping trout forget about their surroundings because they are almost in a trance as they feed on the drifting duns and spinners. I often approach Trico trout from the side. I use extreme caution when doing so and try to get some cover—tall grass or a bush—between me and the trout. I also kneel or crawl to the edge of the stream if I'm fish-

ing from the bank. I keep my movements to a minimum and, if wading, move slowly.

For tippet-shy trout, you may have better luck with a downstream presentation. Cautiously get into position above the rising trout, keeping all movement to an absolute minimum. Cast your fly slightly above the rising trout on a slack line and allow it to drift down into the trout's feeding position so that the fish sees your fly before it sees the tippet.

As the weather turns colder, spinnerfalls become lighter and later in the day. Most anglers fail

Tricos provide dependable fishing into the fall, until the first frost. JACK HANRAHAN PHOTO

to notice that Tricos are even hatching. On autumn days, I've seen good clouds of spinners that did not begin to fall to the water until after the noon hour. Air temperature determines when. My advice is to check your weather channel the night before—or simply show up early and enjoy a cup of coffee along the stream while you wait for nature's dance to unfold.

I usually fish a Snowshoe Trico Emerger when duns are hatching in the morning. These simple-to-tie spinner patterns have worked all over the United States. The only change is in the wing. Have different styles of wings. The poly yarn wings stand up a bit more in the surface film, which helps with seeing the little Trico imitation. On those days when the trout want something lower in the surface, use a pattern with Krystal Flash or CDC wings. If a fish rises to your fly but you fail to hook it, rest the trout and follow up with another fly.

Female Trico Spinner

Hook:	#18-24 Orvis 4641 (1X wide, 1X fine, big eye)
Thread:	White 8/0
Tail:	White hackle four times the length of the hook shank
Body:	Tying thread
Wing:	White poly yarn, white CDC, or pearl Krystal Flash
Thorax:	Black Fine and Dry

Male Trico Spinner

Hook:	#18-24 Orvis 4641 (1X wide, 1X fine, big eye)
Thread:	Black 8/0
Tail:	White hackle four times the length of the hook shank
Body:	Black thread
Wing:	White poly yarn, white CDC, or pearl Krystal Flash
Thorax:	Black Fine and Dry

CHAPTER 3

Midges come in a wide variety of colors and sizes, and hatch all year long. When trout are rising, and you can't see any bugs, consider midges.

Midges

Ever happen on trout that seemed to rise for no apparent reason? When you check the water, you find no obvious food to make the fish rise. On many spring creeks, this common occurrence most likely means midges. If you thought you figured out midge fishing one day and expect the following day to be a success, think again. Sometimes it is best to forget what you thought you learned and observe only what is taking place in front of you. Fly fishermen either love or hate fishing midges. I have met some anglers with boxes full of midge patterns and others who won't carry a single one. Still, like it or not, the rewards often make up for midging misery. Most of the time, fishing these small flies is not as hard as it is made out to be.

Midges (order Diptera) are abundant and extremely important on spring creeks. Anglers often use the term midge to describe to any small bug, whether it is a true midge, caddis, or mayfly, and sometimes a small tuft of fur or feather tied on a hook can suffice to imitate any of these. However, on most spring creeks, it's the true midges (primarily in the family Chironomidae) that are most important to anglers, and the most effective designs imitate the primary characteristics of different stages of these insects.

Midges have a complete life cycle: egg, larva, pupa, and adult. Midge larvae are wormlike bottom-dwellers that live in the spaces between the rocks or in leaves and debris. They range in colors from cream to olive to bright red, a color that anglers refer to as bloodworms. When they start to pupate, they release themselves off the bottom and drift downstream with the current. This can happen at any time, but it is more common early and late in the day. At times, a great number of these little midge larvae may be helplessly drifting downstream, and trout take full advantage of this when they do.

As a hatch begins, midge larvae ascend to the surface. You can fish larvae imitations midcurrent on a dropper beneath a dry fly or suspended under a tiny indicator to help you detect the strike. The Yong Special and Yong Flasher in olive, red, and cream are two of my favorite midge larvae imitations that also do double duty as pupae patterns. The Brassie is another pattern that works well as a larva or pupa depending on where you fish it in the water column. In addition to the classic brass color, I use red, green, black, and even chartreuse. Midge larvae come in many different colors. My midge box has #18-22 olive, cream, and red midge larvae, but trout feeding selectively on midges can be frustratingly difficult to catch and may require other colors or pattern styles.

When they hatch, midge pupae ascend to the surface, where the fully developed midge adult struggles free from the pupal shell. Unlike other insects, midge pupae, wiggling as they drift downstream, drift vertically rather than horizontally in the film. The adult takes a while to break through the pupal skin, so it drifts for a long time, becom-

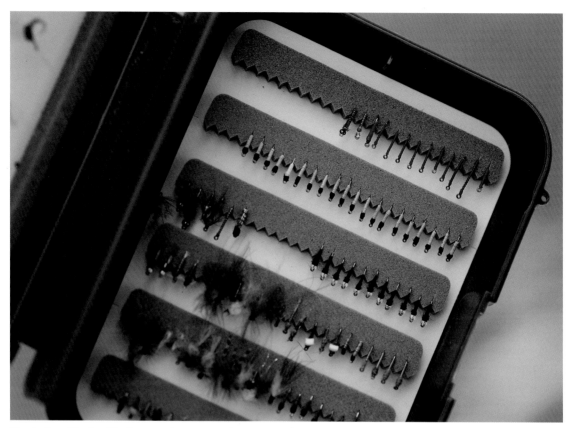

Simple thread-body midge larvae and pupae are often more effective than heavy dressed patterns. Less is more when it comes to imitating midges.

ing vulnerable and easy pickings for trout. Once the adult midge has freed itself from the pupal shell, it quickly flies off the water's surface, sometimes fluttering on the surface as it tries to become airborne.

As more midge pupae fill the surface drift, trout move into feeding lanes, migrating off of the bottom and often holding from inches to a foot below the water's surface. Midge-feeding trout prefer slower currents to avoid expending a lot of energy while feeding, so trout are likely to move into calmer, slower currents along faster runs and riffles or into slow, glassy flats.

Midge pupae drift for a long distance as they struggle out of their pupal skins. Because midge

pupae stay in the film for so long, this stage of the hatch provides the most dependable fishing. Pay close attention to how the trout are feeding. If you see a head roll just below the surface or only the dorsal fin breaking the surface, trout are probably favoring midge pupae. Midge-sipping trout scrutinize every little bit of the fly, so good pupa patterns should have materials that suggest movement, such as CDC or flash, and the patterns should suspend vertically in the film.

To imitate this prominent characteristic of emerging midge pupae, I use a Mike's Midge Pupa, which drifts vertically and has CDC and foam to provide built-in movement and flotation. I have also become fond of the Yong series of midge pupae and some of Don Holbrook's midge patterns. These simple, thread-bodied flies are deadly. Many of these have hints of flash, which can make the patterns more effective in some conditions.

Andy Kim, a guide on the San Juan River in New Mexico, designed the Yong Special to effectively imitate the midge pupa found in abundance on his home waters. Like Don Holbrook, he uses Coats & Clark sewing thread for the body of the fly. Before wrapping the hook, he spins the bobbin to twist the thread, which when wrapped on the shank creates a body with distinct segmentation. For the head he uses black tying thread wrapped so that it is slightly larger than the tho-rax. Head cement is applied to give the head a shiny appearance.

The Yong Flasher is another great midge pupa pattern. It is tied the same as the Yong Special, but it has a little dubbing for the thorax. The variation I tie uses black rabbit dubbing blended with pearl Master Bright Dubbing finely chopped and then spun in a coffee grinder to blend the materials evenly. Determining when to use a Yong Flasher and not a Yong Special is not hard science. If the fish seem spooky, I often go with the more subtle Yong Special, but the subtle flash in the Yong Flasher can be just the ticket for piquing a trout's interest.

This trout took a Yong Blood, which is simply red thread wrapped on a long-shank hook to imitate a midge larva. Red, black, olive, and cream are great colors.

Winter Midge Tactics

Many times, midges are hatching when nothing else is on the water, especially during winter and late fall when all other hatching insects are waiting for warmer air and water temperatures. Surprisingly, winter midge hatches can be heavy, and trout will actively feed on them. During winter, I frequent streams that are pressured during the warmer months, and thanks to midges, I have had some great days on the water.

My friend Shannon Jamison and I hit Big Spring almost every Saturday throughout January and almost always beat the sunrise to ensure that we beat the crowds, even at this time of the year. We like Big Spring because we don't have to cast far, and the limited amount of casting makes for fewer iced guides in the winter. Shannon and I usually start off with a Simple Shrimp or a cress bug tied to 4X tippet and usually land a few trout before any other anglers arrive. One morning we did not do all that well. We could see a few trout feeding inches above the silty bottom, but they passed up our imitations. I headed back to drink another hot cup of coffee and ponder the situation. As I finished my coffee, I noticed hundreds

Even though many anglers say that you should wait and fish during the warmest part of the day during the fall, winter, and early spring, spring creek trout are less affected by air temperatures than trout in freestone streams. Spring creek trout may be rising even with heavy frost on the grass.

of midges gathering on my truck's warm hood. After that clue, we switched over to some #20 red Yong Flashers and found trout eager to take our drifting midge larvae.

Midge larvae imitations can be fished anytime, not just when there is a hatch. If there are no adult midges hatching, dead drift larvae imitations close to the bottom to match the feeble drifting naturals. A tight line dead drift or aid from a small indicator will help you detect the light strikes. One of my favorite ways to fish midge larvae on the bottom is as the second fly in a tandem rig fished under an indicator.

Winter midge tactics are pretty much the same as warm weather tactics, but there are a few winter tricks you should know. Midges often become trapped in the film. Try fishing with lower floating flies like parachutes and lightly dressed CDC midges. Winter midges are most often dark—an adaptation that helps them better absorb the sun's warming rays. Choose a midge that is black, dark olive, or gray. Most hatch activity is from 10:00 AM until 3:00 PM, when the sun is high and day's temperature is highest.

If you fish in the winter, be prepared with extra layers of clothes to keep you warm. Fingerless gloves are a great help. I still favor wool because it stays warm even when wet. If I land a trout or get my wool gloves get wet, I simply ring out the excess water and put them back on. Fleece also has similar qualities. Whatever material you choose, make sure to bring along a spare set of gloves as a backup. Many anglers will tuck a thin pair of glove liners in one of their vest pockets as an emergency backup. These liners do not take up much space.

If it is below freezing, your guides will ice up. There are pastes on the market that you can rub on your guides to prevent ice buildup (or you can use Vaseline), but eventually you'll get ice in your guides. To melt off ice, dip your rod in the water or wrap your warm hands around the ice until it melts. If you use a lot of roll casts and always cast the same amount of line, you can limit the amount of line

When you fish in the winter, wear layers and bring along an extra pair of gloves.

that you have to retrieve through the guides. When you catch a fish, land the trout with or without net, but make sure that you keep it in the water. Any exposure to the freezing air temperature can immediately harm the trout. So quickly take the fly out and release the trout as quickly as possible.

When you are walking along snowy banks, be careful of muskrat holes and other hidden pitfalls. Snow builds up on felt soles in the snow, making it difficult and awkward to walk, so rubber soles such as Aquastealth are better for walking in the snow. Make sure that you have a change of clothes in your vehicle in case you do take a spill. Most of the time my car is nearby, and I'll frequently return to it to have a drink of coffee and warm up.

Yong Special

Hook:	#16-24 Orvis 4641 (1X wide, 1X fine, big eye)
Thread:	Black 8/0
Body:	Coats & Clark All Purpose Dual Duty sewing thread
Thorax:	Black thread

Yong Flasher

Hook:	#16-24 Orvis 4641 (1X wide, 1X fine, big eye)
Thread:	Black 8/0
Body:	Coats & Clark All Purpose Dual Duty sewing thread
Thorax:	Black rabbit and pearl Master Bright Dubbing blend

As the midge hatch continues, some trout follow the midges to the surface and break the surface with head-to-tail rises. Large fish often dimple the surface of the water when they take a midge, which is a riseform often referred to as a sip. When midge activity is heavy, trout often feed repeatedly, pause, and feed again, usually rising two or three times before resting. Because they are stationed close to the surface and feeding heavily, you can get closer to them than if they were holding in deep water and on the lookout for predators. Depending on the stream, many different colors of midges can be hatching simultaneously. To make your decisions more complicated, one trout may be taking adults trying to get airborne while his buddy downstream is feeding on pupae.

At this point in the game, you should present your fly without drag and with the lightest tippet possible that allows you to land the trout efficiently. I often use 7X. Trout are not going to move more than a few inches to take a midge, so place your fly pattern no more than twelve inches above or just to the side of the rising trout. Casting patterns too far above a trout gives it more time to study it. The fly may also begin to drag as it reaches the trout's position. The drag may not be apparent to you, but the trout notices it. If the fish refuses the pattern, wait until you see the trout rise again before making another cast. If the trout doesn't move for your fly, try a few more times because it may not have seen it. Your casts must be extremely accurate when midge fishing.

If you did see the fly float directly over the trout or it followed the pattern and refused it, go with another color or change size. It is hard to fathom, but a single hook size can make a difference when you are midge fishing. Trout notice the slightest size difference, and that is why most midge anglers fail to fool midge-sipping trout. Most of my midge patterns start at #22 and shrink to #28. Many fly fishermen are reluctant to tie on small flies because they can't see them on the water, but buying or tying flies with an orange wing post or tuft of white CDC in the pattern can help you see them better. The best thing to do, though not always possible, is to get as close as possible to the fish so that you can see your fly. Try to stalk the trout and fish the patterns no more than twenty or thirty feet away from you.

Round out your midge box with some winged adults, though they are not as important as emerging pupae. Griffith's Gnats are fine for streams with light angling pressure, and I always carry some to imitate either individual or clusters of midges. For trout that are more pressured, I use a midge with a CDC wing. The CDC can be gray for a natural look or white to help you see it better. CDC midges ride lower in the film and do double duty as pupal and adult imitations. Paramidges such as the ICSI (I Can See It) Midge are easy to see with a post tied with fluorescent orange or yellow.

Even when other insects are on the water, trout sometimes feed exclusively on midges and will refuse all other fly patterns, especially on heavily pressured streams. Because of this, even when you see mayflies or caddis flitting in the air, watch the water to note the fish's riseforms and whether there are also midges around. On one trip to New York, I approached a nice brown rising along a rocky bank. Because a solid Green Drake hatch was in progress, I had an adult Green Drake dun tied to my 5X tippet, but I noticed this trout was passing up the drakes for something else. Seeing nothing else on the water, I lengthened my leader to 7X and tied on a small #22 gray midge. My midge reached the trout, and without hesitating, the eighteen-inch brown sipped it in. The key is to be patient and then decide what to tie on. The trout will tell you what they want.

In *Midge Magic* (Stackpole Books), Don Holbrook chronicles a dazzling array of sizes and colors of midges found just in a few of his local waters. But even Holbrook brings a little bit of order to his day-to-day midge selection by honing in on a few common sizes and colors for his fishery. Though he admits that he carries a wide range of sizes, he writes, "I normally fish a size 18 midge pupa, on a Mustad 3906B hook, because that's the prevailing size year-round in our area streams. But there are times when a smaller size is not only advisable, but almost imperative, if you wish to pick up more than the occasional fish. Over the years, I've finally settled on size 24, on a Mustad 94840 hook, as the other prevailing size pupa. I can't see carrying all the patterns in sizes 18 through 28, although at times I've come close to doing just that. Why complicate life more than it already is?"

No doubt, your fisheries will be different than Holbrook's (two of his testing grounds were Big Spring and the Yellow Breeches, which happen to be two of the toughest midge fisheries around), but once you learn to match the predominate sizes in your stream, your fly selection should be relatively manageable. Even minute size differences can be important, but if you skip a few of the middle sizes, it's probably not the end of the world, especially if you tie some of your #18s short and your #24s long.

In addition to coming in all sorts of sizes, midges also come in a wide variety of colors. Seining the water for specimens is always best, but if you can't do that, try what I have done over the years when I have not been able to determine the exact color of the midge that is emerging. Because midges that hatch in cold weather have dark bodies to absorb sunlight and help them keep warm, from December through April, I start with dark gray, black, or dark olive midge patterns. As the warmer months approach, midges are lighter in color because they need not rely on the sun's warmth to live. So in May through July, I start off with midge patterns in light olive, tan, or light gray and add cream to my box. From July into October, I add white. October becomes the transition month, so from then on, I go with gray and olive patterns first, changing flies if the fish refuse my pattern. If my pattern is refused once again, I change color or fly pattern until I get it right.

Mike's Midge Pupa

I love the challenge of midge fishing. On any given day, different sizes and colors of midges can hatch simultaneously. Observing a feeding trout, choosing a fly, changing the fly more than once if needed, and tying it to fine tippet takes effort, but watching a trout inhale the fly is ample reward.

Unfortunately, that doesn't always happen. I can remember working upstream one day when I found a trout surface-feeding on midges. After a careful approach, I was ready to cast. I waited and watched. The trout's feeding behavior revealed that he was sipping on a midge pupa. I tied a Brassie to my 7X tippet—no luck. Next, a black midge pupa—refused again. That trout was one up on me that day, but I wouldn't forget him.

In the following days, I thought about that fish. Those patterns had worked before, but why not

on him? I realized that the problem may have been with how the pattern floated in the water. A natural midge pupa floats vertically rather than horizontally. I dropped the Brassie and the others in a glass, and when I saw that they suspended horizontally in the water, I went straight for my fly-tying vise.

The key features to a midge pupa are the abdomen, thorax, and moving gills. The abdomen has prominent segmentation, so I elected to tie it from goose biots. I needed a material to imitate the moving gills that would float. Cul-de-canard (CDC) came to mind. It is delicate, it can mimic tiny movements, and its natural oils make this material as buoyant as cork. Excited at the possibilities, I quickly made the thorax from peacock herl and thought I had my fly.

This wild brown took a Mike's Midge Pupa when all other patterns failed. Even though midges were not hatching at the time, the trout sucked in this small, unobtrusive pattern because it looked like something familiar.

During the winter, midges are the main game if you want to catch trout on the surface.

When I dropped my creation into a glass of water, I was unhappy with the results. The CDC didn't keep the fly afloat. I knew the material I used for the thorax must aid the CDC, and finding it took some time and much trial and error. I came across a sheet of black foam and thought a thin strip tied in overlapping wraps might help the CDC. I grabbed my glass of water and tried it. It was a beautiful sight. The CDC and foam combination floated the fly well, and the body hung beneath the surface exactly like a live midge pupa.

Even though I wanted to go after the Falling Spring rainbow that drove me to create a better pattern, I first tested my Mike's Midge Pupa on the Yellow Breeches. As I tied the pupa to my tippet with a clinch knot, I felt like a kid at Christmas. Several casts and several released browns later, I knew this fly was going to work well for me. Over the years, this fly has caught trout on all water I have fished, and I credit the creation of this fly to that 16-3/4-inch Falling Spring rainbow, which I later caught with it.

Mike's Midge Pupa

Hook:	#18-22 Orvis 4641 (1X wide, 1X fine, big eye)
Thread:	Gray 8/0
Abdomen:	Olive, gray, or brown goose biot
Thorax:	Thin strip of black foam ($1/16$ inch thick)
Gills:	White CDC for visibility; gray CDC for a more natural look

Reading the Rise

Vince Marinaro, in *A Modern Dry Fly Code,* goes into depth about the riseforms and concludes trout will rise in three ways: a simple rise, a compound rise, and the complex rise. Marinaro also writes that fly fishers should determine whether the trout is taking the fly off or in the surface film by watching for water disturbance. Understanding riseforms is important, particularly when you are facing several insect species on the water at once.

The most common rise I encounter on spring creeks is the sip rise, where the trout's nose just breaks through the water's surface as it takes the fly. Usually, larger floating mayflies and caddis can be seen disappearing into the trout's mouth. Sips can also occur when trout are taking midges, terrestrials, and spent spinners. If you do not see any insects, then the trout may be on small terrestrials or emergers.

The classic head-to-tail rise probably signals trout are feeding on small insects such as midges, small Blue-Winged Olives and other small mayflies, microcaddis, or small terrestrials. This is one of the easiest riseforms to see, which in turn makes it much easier to cast your fly accurately. Head-to-tail rising trout are often selective, so be ready for a battle of wits.

For me, a boil rise is the most exciting, and it is usually is accompanied by considerable surface disturbance. Here the trout are often keying on large mayflies or caddis. Boils can also mean a trout has taken, and is on the lookout for, larger terrestrials like crickets or hoppers.

Bulge rises often go unnoticed. The trout does not break the water's surface; it often just pushes the water's film. The bulge is usually an indication that the trout is feeding on midges or small mayflies just below the surface as they are emerging.

The gulping rise indicates the trout are feeding heavily on a hatch or spinnerfall. The gulp is a head rise sucking down many bugs at one time. The gulping trout may even swim upstream, head out of water, sink back below the surface, and drift back downstream. Just like head-to-tail rising trout, these trout are spooky, so watch your cast and approach.

Once I observe the riseform, I move downstream of the rising trout to see if any insects are drifting by, then collect what may be hatching and match size and color accordingly. If I know I'm in the ballpark and the fly was refused, it just may be a simple pattern change. Knowing what to tie to the tippet is part of the game, and the other part is presentation.

Sipping riseforms are classic indications of a trout feeding on midges.

Armstrong's Spring Creek, near Livingston, Montana, has intense midge hatches. JOHN RANDOLPH PHOTO

CDC Adult Midge

Hook: #18-22 Orvis 4641 (1X wide, 1X fine, big eye)

Thread: Gray 8/0 or color to match body

Abdomen: Gray, olive, black, brown, tan, or white Fine and Dry

Wing: White or gray CDC

Head: Thread

Note: The CDC floats well and will move while on the surface. The fly rides low in the water. When dressing CDC with dry-fly floatant, always use a powder floatant. Spray, gel, or liquid dry-fly floatant will destroy the natural buoyancy of the CDC feather.

Light equipment and long leaders add to the difficult demands of midge fishing. Long, fine leaders are required to accompany such frail little patterns, and I may fish a leader as long as 11 to 13 feet with 7X tippet. Some die-hard midge fishermen up the ante by using tippets lighter than 7X, but for me, 7X is it, and if the midge battle ends in my defeat, well, there will be another day. For most of my midge fishing, I use a soft- to medium-action three-weight to help protect the delicate tippets and provide a softer presentation. Every cast must be perfect, every time, and the fly must land on the mark so that it floats directly to the sipping trout. The long leader must roll over and break down in S curves as it settles to the surface.

CHAPTER 4

Skating a caddis on the surface draws splashy rises, even on the placid currents of a spring creek. This wild brown fell for a deer-hair caddis just before dark. JACK HANRAHAN PHOTO

Caddis and Stoneflies

While anglers have mostly overlooked caddisflies throughout fly-fishing history, you can be sure that trout haven't. Caddisflies play such a significant role in trout's diets that studies have shown they make up almost half of all aquatic food trout consume in some streams. Why have fly fishermen ignored caddisfly hatches for all these years?

For a long time, far too much angling focus and reading material emphasized mayflies. Although some authors, such as Solomon and Leiser in *The Caddis and the Angler*, were writing about the importance of these insects, for the most part, little literature that was accessible for anglers explained the importance of caddisflies in a trout's diet. One of the most important contributions to caddisfly literature came with the publication of *Caddisflies*, written by Gary LaFontaine, which is still the best book on the subject. Now, fly fishers have come to realize that several caddis species are extremely important to trout and seek these hatches out.

But even as freestone anglers have come around and begun to understand the importance of caddis, spring creek anglers are just beginning to embrace these bugs. Gary LaFontaine writes in *Caddisflies*, "For some reason caddisflies have never been strongly linked with spring creeks. In all the books and articles extolling the special kind of fly-fishing experiences provided by these streams there is very little about the magnificent caddisfly hatches. There can no longer be any excuse for ignoring

the fine fly-fishing available at these times." Caddisflies are a very important part of the fish's diet, and an important part of the menu of an angler's year on a spring creek. Certain species such as Black Caddis, Grannoms, and microcaddis provide first-rate dry-fly fishing opportunities.

All caddis species have a one-year life cycle and, unlike mayflies, undergo complete metamorphosis: egg, larva, pupa, and adult. Caddis larvae make up a good percentage of the food consumed by trout. Pick up a few rocks, and you will see several different caddis larvae: free living, purse-case makers, and tube-case makers. Free-living caddis larvae have a caterpillar shape, six well-developed legs, dark heads, and green, off-white, tan, or light orange bodies, with shades of green the most common. These caddisflies rely on cool, well-oxygenated waters and cling to rocks and sticks within riffles. A simple green dubbed body with a peacock herl head suffices as a general, all-purpose pattern for this almost ubiquitous insect. The abdomen color of this fly pattern can be changed to match other free-living caddis. I tie them in yellow, off-white, and pale pink.

Purse-case makers live as free-living caddis for much of their larval life and then build a case around themselves when they are ready to pupate. Microcaddis fall into the super group of purse-case makers. They live as free-living caddis for much of their larval life and inconspicuously crawl along the bottom. Microcaddis can be found living in the riffles of the streams where flows are

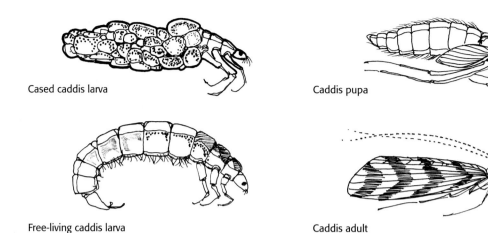

Cased caddis larva

Caddis pupa

Free-living caddis larva

Caddis adult

RICK TAKAHASHI ILLUSTRATIONS

greater and water is more oxygenated. Prior to pupation, the microcaddis build meshlike nets around themselves and quickly increase in size and gain strength. These shelters are flatter in appearance, hence the name "purse case." Shelters are made from woven silk, vegetation, or stones and expand as the larvae grow.

The most highly evolved of the caddis larvae are the tube-case makers. These caddis larvae are easily recognized by the case made from tiny pebbles, small sticks, and even shredded sticks and leaves around their caterpillar-like bodies. These cases are not just used as homes but are well adapted for camouflage, water circulation, and buoyancy.

When the larvae are ready to pupate, they fully enclose themselves in their cases, and if they don't have a case, they make one for pupation. If you notice caddis larvae enclosed in their cases, a hatch is only days away. Once pupation is complete, the fully developed, winged caddis tears out of the shelter and rises to the surface. When the caddis breaks through the case, its protective pupal sheath slowly starts to fill with gas. At this stage the insect is an adult caddis fully equipped to fly away, but it must reach the water's surface. So the pupal skin becomes the protective barrier, aiding the adult caddis in its rise to the water's surface. Upon ap-

proaching the surface film, the caddis begins to tear out of the pupal skin. Once free, the adult caddis may ride on the surface briefly or immediately take to the air, depending on the species.

In a few days, the caddis mate and the females begin laying eggs, either depositing their eggs on the surface of the water or diving into the water and depositing their eggs below the surface. To imitate an adult, egg-laying caddis swimming through the water to deposit her eggs, you need to fish your flies differently than if you are imitating a species of caddis that lays its eggs on the surface.

Fishing the Caddis

Each stage of caddis development is an important food source for the trout. Most nymph fishermen rely on mayfly nymphs and crustacean patterns and fail to realize the importance of caddisfly larvae in trout's diets. Trout poke their noses at rocks and underwater vegetation as they try to root out insects such as caddis in a feeding behavior called grubbing. Anglers can pick out grubbing trout by the distinct silvery flashes seen underwater, caused by the trout's struggle to keep in the feeding position. Trout also feed on caddis larvae drifting in the current. They find a good feeding station, generally in calm water, and swim side to side to intercept larvae as they drift by.

Fish eat most caddis larvae within one foot of the stream's bottom, and that's where you should fish your imitations. Trout generally ignore flies drifting too high because they look unnatural. When I spot a trout, I get as close as possible to the fish and high-stick my pattern with a dead drift. I try to position myself to see the take, but if I can't spot a fish, I work the seams and edges along faster runs and riffles or fish around any rocks or structures that could possibly hold trout. I often fish a tandem rig with bead and beadless versions of the same fly or two different patterns.

Taking a cue from Gary LaFontaine, I think of caddis hatches in three stages: deep pupa, emergent pupa, and adult. When larvae are ready to pupate, they immediately begin to fill their transparent sheaths with air and the bubbles reflect sunlight, sparkling in the water. Trout may key on this characteristic and become selective to it. Patterns should imitate or collect tiny air bubbles like the natural.

My mainstay pupae patterns are LaFontaine's Deep Sparkle Pupae and Emergent Sparkle Pupae.

Even if you are casting upstream and allowing the caddis to drift over the trout, a subtle twitch of the fly can be just what it takes to trigger a take.

You can tie LaFontaine's pioneering patterns in just about any color combination possible since Antron comes in just about every color. It's a complex tie, at least for me, but the results are worth it. The touched-dubbed Antron budding and veiling of Antron trap bubbles unlike no other pattern I've tried. The Deep Sparkle Pupae is heavily weighted to be fished on the bottom and the Emergent Sparkle Pupae has a pinch of deer hair to help it ride higher in the currents. For complete tying instructions, check out *Caddisflies.*

Soft-hackles can work well because they also collect bubbles, and the fibers move as the fly drifts in the water. Some caddis pupae crawl out of the water to emerge. To match this, try a down-and-across cast. Allow the fly to reach the bottom and lift as it gets closer to the stream bank.

As the caddis pupae break out of their cocoons, they drift helplessly in the currents until gas fills their pupal skins, which helps them rise to the surface. During this stage, trout feed along the bottom on these drifting pupae. To catch these fish, you can dead drift a Deep Sparkle Pupa or lightly dressed soft-hackle tight to the bottom.

As more and more caddis pupae enter the surface drift, hungry trout begin to follow the emerging pupae up from the stream's bottom. At this point, a dead drift generally becomes ineffective. To imitate swimming and crawling pupae, you can use several techniques. One way is with a down-and-across cast to mimic a pupa's trip from the bottom to the surface. For this, I use the Emergent Sparkle Pupa or a soft-hackle fished across and downstream so that it swings in front of the feeding trout. Because the line is tight, just lift your rod to set the hook. It takes some practice. Many times you have a little too much line out, the fly swings behind the trout, and you line the fish. It's better to cast well upstream of the fish and slowly step down or make longer casts until the fly swings in front of the fish.

You can also imitate the pupa by positioning yourself directly across from your target. Cast your fly upstream of the trout and then start lifting your rod a hair faster than the current as the fly drifts downstream. Let the fly swing across the stream once it passes in front of you, and you might be rewarded with a strike.

The Leisenring lift works well in slower pools and flats, and though it usually requires that you approach closely to a feeding trout that you have spotted, you can also use it as a searching tactic through good-looking water. Let the fly sink, drifting downstream on a slack line with the rod tip pointing at the fly at all times. As the drowned fly reaches the intended target, stop following the fly with the rod tip so the fly begins to drag and rises through the water column to the surface. The sudden swing of the fly to the surface, if timed so that it occurs when the fish can see it, is a strong trigger for them to take your fly.

If I don't spot any trout, I fish the water with these same techniques, but in steps. If I'm working a length of stream from above, I start at the top of a riffle or flat. I cast across and allow my fly to swing across the surface. I watch where my fly has swung across the stream. Next, I cautiously take one step downstream or cast another foot of line, and I continue this approach until I've covered the entire run. I have found that if I work downstream in one-foot increments, I'm less likely to line a trout. I do the same thing if I am working across the stream or casting upstream using the Leisen-

Soft-hackles make excellent imitations of emerging pupae. Other good patterns are LaFontaine's Sparkle series.

ring lift. I either move downstream a foot at a time or simply cast more line.

A good dry-fly leader with a fine tippet is essential to get drag-free floats. I use the George Harvey leader formula, tapering it down to 28 inches of 6X or 7X, depending on the size of the caddis adult imitation. I normally use 6X when I'm fishing patterns on hooks in sizes of 14 and 16. For me, size 18 is the dividing line. If the trout are tippet-shy, I use 7X; if not, I stick with the heavier tippet. Anything under a size 20 gets a tippet of 7X.

Caddis are not on the water's surface as long as mayflies. During the hatch, the pupa pauses just under the surface for a brief period. Once the adult emerges, it flutters its wings and quickly flies away. As a result, there aren't that many caddis drifting serenely on the water's surface. Adult caddis head right to streamside vegetation where they congregate low and close to the water's surface. They can live for several weeks until it is time to lay their eggs.

Though many adult caddis are best imitated with a more active retrieve, spent egg-laying caddis provide a superb opportunity to dead drift caddis patterns such as Lawson's Spent Partridge Caddis. Gary LaFontaine describes these egg-laying caddis as passive egg layers. These female caddis quietly ride on the surface after depositing their eggs. Here standard dead-drift dry-fly tactics work well.

But caddis egg layers also flop around on the water as they lay their eggs, and to imitate these cases, you need to put your dry fly, such as a Dancing Caddis or Elk Hair Caddis, into motion as it drifts. Carry patterns that lie flush in the film to imitate spent caddis and have some hackled ones on hand to skate and twitch on the water's surface to imitate any active egg layers. Watch the naturals and choose your patterns accordingly. Riseforms can also be an important clue. If you hear splashy rises, trout are chasing something; sippy rises often mean the prey is not going anywhere fast.

Whether you are skating a caddis or fishing it drag-free, you need a long leader and a well-dressed fly. JACK HANRAHAN PHOTO

Black Caddis, Grannoms, and Microcaddis

Many different caddis can be locally important, but the three most important spring creek caddis on the waters that I fish are Black Caddis, Grannoms, and various species of microcaddis—Grannoms and microcaddis are also extremely important on Western spring creeks. Both Black Caddis and Grannoms hatch when warm spring temperatures

Black Caddis live in trout streams in the East and Midwest and are one of the first trout stream insects to hatch.

settle over the stream. When stream temperatures begin to rise, so do the appetites of the trout. Microcaddis are often overlooked by anglers, but they are abundant in many spring creeks, widespread, and provide dependable fishing.

Black Caddis (*Chimarra aterimma*), also called Little Black Sedges, are a hearty species dispersed over a large region and a wide variety of streams in the East and Midwest. Members of the Philopotamidae family, Chimarra species (which also includes *C. obscura* and *C. socia,* according to LaFontaine) do not build cases but instead build nets on the undersides of rocks that filter small particles of food from the current. LaFontaine's Yellow Caddis Larva or a small, yellow soft-hackle makes a good match for the naturals.

Before hatching, Black Caddis larvae seal their shelters and transform into pupae, a process that usually takes about two weeks. If you see Black Caddis sealed in cases, some caddis will be hatching soon. Most of the Black Caddis pupae crawl to shallow edges, where they emerge from the water as adults. When mature, the pupa breaks through the enclosed case to ascend to the water's surface. LaFontaine's Sparkle Pupae and soft-hackles with blended Antron yarn bodies trap air bubbles and reflect light like the naturals. As the emerging caddis reach the surface, the fully developed caddis break through their pupal skins to emerge as winged adults.

The first time I saw a Black Caddis hatch was on one of my favorite beats on Falling Spring Branch. I was coming up on the Rose Bush Hole when I noticed black spots all over the bright green meadow grass. At first I thought it was some type of grass disease. I cautiously approached this tiny riffle and noticed that the little black spots were moving. As I got even closer, I could see that the bank was black with caddis, and a few trout at the head of the riffle were actively working back and forth. I nipped off my cress bug and tied on a small wet fly, which proved to be the right move.

Anglers should begin looking for Black Caddis emergences starting in April lasting into July, with the hatches starting around 11:00 AM daily and generally over by 4:00 PM. In most cases, once Black Caddis have emerged, they take to the air with a flutter or two and retreat to streamside vegetation. They are on the water only for a brief period during the hatch. Trout have few opportunities to take adults from the surface because the adults immediately try to leave the water. Most fly fishermen pass up the midday festivities to focus on the evening event.

However, there are often enough little Black Caddis on the water to make a few trout rise. In these instances, there may be some crippled Black Caddis floating helplessly on the surface, which makes for good dry-fly fishing. A #16-20 Elk Hair Caddis along with 36 inches of 6X tippet often works, and sometimes I like to use a black CDC Caddis to imitate the dainty struggle associated with cripples.

After several days, Black Caddis adults begin swarming above the water to mate. At dusk, incredible numbers of females start peppering the water, depositing their eggs, and dying. This is tailormade dry-fly fishing and the most exciting time to take advantage of this hatch. At dusk, the egg-laying females hit the water to deposit their eggs, where trout gorge on them. When Black Caddis fall, they generally ride on the surface of the water for a long time, making for great dry-fly fishing.

Black Elk Hair Caddis

Hook: #16-20 Orvis 4641 (1X wide, 1X fine, big eye)
Thread: Black 8/0
Body: Black Fine and Dry
Hackle: Palmered black hackle
Wing: Black elk hair

Note: Thread, body, hackle, and wing color can be changed to match natural

Black CDC Caddis

Hook: #14-20 Orvis 4641 (1X wide, 1X fine, big eye)
Thread: Black 8/0
Body: Black Fine and Dry
Underwing: Gray Z-lon
Wing: Dark gray CDC

Note: Can also be used to imitate black stonefly hatches

If fish are particular about size, I'll first collect a few drifting naturals to get an exact match. I then let the trout choose the pattern to accompany the tippet. I will use a black Elk Hair Caddis if the trout are keying on caddis floating high on the surface. Trout feeding on sinking, egg-laying caddis or Black Caddis that are twitching slightly will get a black CDC Caddis drifted over their noses. The CDC wing effectively mimics the gentle struggle sometimes associated with egg-laying females. If trout are still rising at dusk, I switch to a small Elk Hair Caddis, which floats high and is easier to see than the CDC Caddis.

The American Grannom (*Brachycentrus* species) cause trout to go crazy. Eastern fly fishermen typically call this super caddis "Grannoms." They usually begin to appear on eastern streams by mid-April and last for several weeks. Western anglers know it as the Mother's Day Caddis, though on hallowed Grannom waters such as the Yellowstone, Mother's Day is a little late—the hatch gets going by the second or third week in April, just before the warmer weather also brings runoff. Grannoms have olive bodies and speckled, brownish tan wings. They are widely distributed from coast to coast and live in a broad range of waters, from small spring creeks to large streams.

I can still remember my first Grannom experience. It was a cool mid-April day, and as expected,

The American Grannom, also called the Mother's Day Caddis, is often one of the first blizzard hatches of the year.

an above-average crowd of anglers was fishing the one-mile special-regulated section of the Yellow Breeches at the Allenberry Playhouse. The hatch began around 10:00 AM. By 10:30 AM the surface and air were saturated with Grannoms. My waders were covered with pupal shucks. As the hatch strengthened, the formerly quiet and calm surface erupted with rising trout. Trout rose with heavy splashes, and I could see others slashing inches beneath the surface. Some trout leaped out of the water as they chased their escaping meals. Unfortunately, I became frustrated as my fly drifted over the nutty trout without a hit. But as time passed, the aggressive trout soon destroyed my olive deer hair caddis.

Grannom caddis larvae build around themselves chimneylike cases made from plant material or tiny pebbles. They attach themselves to rock or wood debris, sometimes stacked two or three high, with a gluelike substance. This stick case presents some fly design challenges. I have dabbled with fine sand and thinly sliced toothpicks glued to lead-wrapped bodies, but the patterns were tedious to tie and hard to cast; they probably made better paperweights. Eventually, I settled on a simple clipped-hen-hackle pattern with a small orange head as an effective case-caddis pattern.

Grannom caddis drift along in the currents until their pupal skin fills with gas. When that occurs, a soft-hackle or LaFontaine's Deep Sparkle

When I am not sight-fishing, I often fish a caddis over a promising lie.

Pupa will fool trout inhaling the helplessly drifting pupae. I fish these patterns dead drift along the bottom. Once the pupal skins have filled with gas, the Grannom pupae take a quick ride to the surface, where they spend a good deal of time in the surface film as they struggle to break free from their pupal skin. Riseforms are usually aggressive because the trout are slashing back and forth as they gulp down the drifting pupae. This is a good time to fish a LaFontaine's Emergent Sparkle Pupa or a soft-hackle.

As afternoon approaches and the sun lowers in the sky, the female Grannoms start to return to the water to lay their eggs. A few start at first, followed by more, until the surface becomes littered with egg-laying females. Some fall spent on the surface, and others take more of a dive-bomb approach. When they dive bomb, they are trying to swim underwater to deposit their eggs. Once finished they will rise and drift in or on the surface. You can fish this dead drift or with an active retrieve. Let the fish tell you what they prefer.

The females' return sparks a feeding frenzy. Awaiting trout start to rise, filling their bellies with dying Grannoms. As surface numbers grow, so does the number of rising trout. When both spent and sunken caddis are on the water simultaneously, you might find that casting the same pattern to all the fish rising around you is not effective. Observation will pay big dividends at this point. Pick out a trout and watch what it is doing. Is the trout gulping down high-floating Grannoms, or does it just push the surface with a dimple rise? If the rise is more noticeable or you see the trout break the surface, go with a higher floating imitation like an Elk Hair Caddis.

Trout rising to sunken or diving caddis complicate things. The diving caddis baffled fly fishermen for many years. But thanks to Larry Solomon and Solomon's Diving Caddis, anglers became more successful when trout were feeding lower in the film. I have also had good luck with a simple CDC Caddis when trout are looking lower in the

water surface or keying on a subtle movement from dying caddis.

Beadhead Green Caddis Larva

Hook:	#14-16 Orvis 62KC or other continuous bend, 1X short, 2X heavy hook
Thread:	Black 8/0
Ribbing:	Small copper wire
Body:	Olive Wapsi Hare's Ear Dubbing
Thorax:	Natural Hare's Ear dubbing
Head:	Gold, copper, or black bead

Stoneflies

Starting in winter and lasting until early spring (early April) many spring creeks have hatches of small, black stoneflies. My use of the words "small black stoneflies" is descriptive rather than intended to be associated with any particular species, common names for which range from Little Black Stoneflies to Early Black Stoneflies to Early Dark Stoneflies. These common names can be hard to untangle because all of these winter stoneflies come early in the trout fishing season; all of them are small, ranging from slender little 3/8-inch to 3/4-inch-long insects; and all are black, or at least dark brown. These stoneflies belong to the families Taeniopterygidae, Nemouridae, Capniidae, and

Microcaddis

Microcaddis fall into the family of purse-case makers. On many spring creeks, these tiny caddis are abundant and an important part of the trout's diet. Early on, I mistook these caddis for little Black Caddis larvae, but I later learned these dense populations of microcaddis commonly live beneath rocks in the more turbulent stretches of spring creeks. The most common colors are speckled tan and gray, but you may encounter other important colors.

Because they are small (#18-22), many times a midge larva pattern will suffice. In fact, Gary LaFontaine hints in *Caddisflies* that perhaps the effectiveness of the popular Colorado pattern, the Brassie, is due to the glints of flash in the cases of many caddisfly larvae, including microcaddis. Whatever the reason, the Brassie is undoubtedly an effective spring creek fly, and microcaddis are abundant.

Microcaddis hatch from June through September on many Eastern and Western spring creeks. Before emerging, microcaddis build a case around themselves, within which they develop into full-winged adults. When it is time to emerge, these tiny caddis break through their enclosed cocoons and ascend to the surface. Once on the surface, microcaddis begin tearing through the pupal skin.

This rainbow ate a microcaddis fished on a 16-inch dropper below a Letort Cricket. MIKE HECK PHOTO

Leuctridae, and probably others that I am not aware of. The scientific classification is messy, and not all that important as far as fishing the bugs is concerned, since the nymphal and adult stages of these little blacks can be matched with all of the same imitations, and the fishing methods used to imitate the naturals' behavior is similar.

The insect photographer Thomas Ames devotes the last page of his book *Fishbugs* (Countryman Press) to the winter stoneflies, but for Ames, these early black stones are just "a promise of spring," and do not provide any real fishing opportunity: "No, the winter stoneflies are not a sign that it is time to go fishing, or even that the long winter is finally over. They are more like the New England fly fisher's equivalent of the woodchuck that appears each February 2 in Pennsylvania . . . to tell us what we already know, that there will be six more weeks of winter." This may be the case on the free-stone waters of New England, but on spring creeks (and tailwaters) in Pennsylvania, Maryland, Virginia, and New York, the emergences of tiny black stoneflies can mean some great fly fishing action. On many spring creeks, small black stoneflies hatch from December through March, ranging from the tiny Capniidae family (*Allocapnia* and *Capnia*, some anglers call these "snowflies") that hatch on warm days in January to the larger (though still small)

They may tear through their pupal skin rather quickly or drift some distance before successfully breaking free. Rising trout are often mistaken to be taking midges because these caddis are so small. Rises are usually dainty, much like a trout sipping midges, and many midge imitations are probably taken for minute caddis.

Writing of *Agraylea multipunctata*, common name Salt and Pepper Microcaddis, Gary LaFontaine states, "In weedy spring creeks, from Hat Creek in California to the Letort Spring Run in Pennsylvania, the crippled adults and pupae from the nighttime activity, plus a few fresh stragglers, are nearly always on the water at dawn during June and July. The trout lay at the edges of the weeds and sip these caddisflies steadily and quite selectively for the first hour of daylight." LaFontaine recommends #20-24 Lawson's Spent Partridge Caddis to imitate the adults, and I've had good luck with tiny CDC caddis or other downwing patterns in colors and sizes to match the natural.

Microcaddis dive into the water to deposit their eggs, a behavior that can be matched by fishing soft-hackles or LaFontaine's Diving Caddis. You can fish these flies upstream with a dead drift or

Microcaddis larvae can be imitated with your regular larvae patterns, just size them down.

with the traditional down-and-across presentation, either alone or in a tandem rig with other patterns. My primary microcaddis larvae imitations are just smaller versions of larger caddis larvae tied on #16-20 hooks with or without a beaded head. Bright green is my favorite color; however, I do tie imitations with yellow, olive, and pink bodies. Any small nymph pattern or soft-hackle may also be mistaken for a microcaddis larva at times.

Taeniopteryx, which begin hatching in February and often continue into April on the Pennsylvania spring creeks.

Those anglers out on the water this early in the season often fail to notice the insects, perhaps thinking that the trout are rising to midges and Blue-Winged Olives. Unseasonably warm days spark not only midge hatches but also good hatches of Black Stoneflies, which have adapted to the cold well enough during early season emergences to keep warm within cavities in snowbanks.

When stoneflies are in flight, you can see both pairs of wings, which helps you distinguish them from other insects. Adult stoneflies are not at home

while flying—in fact, they are clumsy in the air— but they are extremely agile runners. Just try to snatch one off a twig! Winged adults have two short tails and two pairs of wings, which at rest are flat on the body, hence the common name "flatwings."

One January day several years ago, I was fishing one of my favorite spots on the Letort, enjoying the solitude provided by fishing in the dead of winter. I was not expecting much insect activity. There was no snow on the ground, so I felt comfortable sneaking around some of the treacherous muskrat-inhabited banks. It was mild for January; looking back at my stream log, I can tell you it was sunny and 39 degrees F. I was fishing with nymphs

Adult stoneflies that emerge in the winter and early spring provide an abundant food source for trout. Winter black stoneflies can be matched with larger versions of the patterns you use to imitate Black Caddis.

and a few streamers to no avail when, at about 10:00 AM, I noticed a few trout sporadically rising. As they were rising, they were moving left to right. I immediately thought of Black Stoneflies and began to watch the stream for clues. Finally I noticed a few bugs with that distinct sluggish flight and knew for sure they were Black Stoneflies. I lengthened my tippet to 6X, tied on a Black Stonefly dry, and managed to catch one of the three rising browns. Though they were not large by any means—nor was it an epic, you-had-to-be-there hatch—it was a nice experience on a winter day.

Adult stoneflies can live for days to several weeks once they emerge. During this period, black stoneflies spend much of their short adult lives hidden at the base of trees, in undercut banks, or under driftwood, looking for structures that will warm their slender little bodies. So, I explore around stone structures adjacent to a stream, such as bridge pilings, rocks, and old foundations, for signs of a hatch. Because the little black stoneflies are adapted to colder winter emergences, you will probably also see some on snow-covered banks.

Stonefly nymphs dislike all calm water and live in swifter runs, riffles, and heavy pocket water, where they cling to rocks, boulders, and submerged debris. Though the nymphs aren't great swimmers, they are agile crawlers. Turn over a rock in these locations, and you may see many nymphs and larvae meandering around the underside of that rock, but a stonefly nymph will quickly scurry to the dark side of the rock because it does not like the light.

In winter through early spring, I often fish #14-18 black stonefly nymphs dead drift along the bottom, focusing on the faster broken water and passing over long flats and other slow water. In the turbulent currents, takes are usually not subtle. I tie a simple stonefly nymph imitation (with or without a bead) with dark brown to black fur, thick black goose biots for the tail, and an abdomen of wrapped black Ultra Wire. Natural wild turkey tail does a nice job of forming a wing case. You can also use Prince Nymphs and black Hare's Ears in smaller sizes to imitate black stonefly nymphs.

To emerge, which they usually do in the morning, stoneflies crawl from their hiding places to the streamside bank. They climb out of the water and find a suitable rock, tree, or even a piece of driftwood. The stonefly nymph then secretes a gluelike substance to anchor its nymphal skin, and the winged adult eventually breaks free from it. It is sometimes possible to fool a trout into taking stoneflies during the emergence. I try to swing my nymph pattern, almost dragging, as close to the stream bottom as possible. Another possibility is fishing a Leadwing Coachman or similarly effective pattern with a down-and-across technique. It is also effective to work stonefly nymphs along the banks. Sometimes trout follow the emerging nymphs to the banks. This can be an easy meal as the nymphs crawl from the stream. You can present nymph patterns dead drift or slowly swing the nymphs into the bank.

To swing flies toward the bank, I cast toward the center of the stream and then begin to follow the drift, pointing my rod tip at the end of the line as I follow it across current. As the fly begins to swing, I continue to point my tip at the line and slowly lower my rod tip to the water's surface to keep the fly down lower in the current. On smaller creeks, I may use a tight-line technique following the drift down and then across the stream until my line is parallel with the streambank. Again, I keep my rod tip pointed at the line and lower it as it drifts across the stream. When I am searching the water, I step downstream after each cast, making sure to cover likely lies.

The best dry-fly action comes when the females begin to lay their eggs, usually between mid-morning and early afternoon. At this time, the female stoneflies usually fly just above the surface, dipping their eggs into the water. They continue these flights until they have deposited all of their eggs or until an awaiting trout or bird picks them

This nice brown took a large black CDC dry fly fished dead-drift under overhanging alders.

Stoneflies live in the faster stretches of spring creeks. In these areas, a stonefly nymph fished dead-drift can tempt some of the larger trout.

up. The nature of the female's flight makes for a splashy rise. This is good to know because Blue-Winged Olives and midges are often on the water at the same time. Generally, trout take midges and Blue-Winged Olives in more of the classic head-to-tail or tiny "sipping" riseform. A rise to a stonefly is generally more of a gulp that creates a lot of surface disturbance.

Before deciding how to fish your stonefly dry, watch the trout's feeding behavior. If the trout is on station and moving only slightly, fish the stonefly pattern like a standard mayfly pattern. Cast the fly above the rising trout and allow it to drift drag-free. When trout are chasing the flying stoneflies, they create splashy rises or noticeably move from side to side. If they are doing this, cast the fly above the fish—usually two or three feet—and then skip or twitch it on the surface by stripping in an inch or two with about a two-second pause between strips. At times when I'm searching for trout, I'll walk the banks or wade while swinging a stonefly dry downstream and across the surface, especially when covering long flats or gentle riffles. I keep my cast under twenty feet and keep my rod parallel with the water's surface and the rod tip pointed at the fly at all times while following the drift down and across the stream. The stonefly imitation drifts dead for a brief period and then begins to skate across the surface. I have sometimes taken trout that have come several feet to inhale a skating stonefly pattern. Floatant is essential to keep the fly skating. If the pattern sinks, follow through with the drift until the swing is complete—trout will take a sunk pattern as well.

Trout can become less selective to pattern because there is not much food available during the colder months. Still, I do carry a handful of flies for rising trout. On glassy surfaces, I use patterns dressed with two short tails, dubbed bodies, and a dark CDC or deer- or elk-hair wing that lies over the hook shank. In choppier water or when swinging a pattern, I use the same pattern with three wraps of dark dun hackle no longer than

A small Black CDC Caddis cast underneath a low bridge fooled this trout. There were no caddis around, so perhaps the fish took it for a beetle or other terrestrial.

the hook gap on the upper portion of the hook, and over that I tie down a wing similar to a black Elk Hair Caddis. I also sometimes fish a #14-18 black Stimulator.

Stoneflies need well-oxygenated, unpolluted waters to survive, and their presence indicates good water quality. Not that long ago, the hatchery at Big Spring near Newville, Pennsylvania, was shut down for pollution that was killing nearly all the insects that needed the best water quality. One

Dead-drifting a stonefly nymph catches fish in late fall and winter.

year after the hatchery closed, I noticed a significant increase in black stoneflies and better hatches of Blue-Winged Olives.

Though I am not aware of any true spring creeks in the country that have hatches of the large golden stones or Salmonflies, many limestoners and creeks influenced by spring creeks, such as Big Fishing Creek, Yellow Breeches, and Penns Creek, have good populations of golden stones and other stoneflies such as the enormous *Pteronarcys dorsata*, the even-larger Eastern cousin of the Western Salmonfly, and Yellow Sallies. If you are fishing any of these streams, it pays to have some imitations in your box.

Heck's Stonefly Nymph (Brown)

Hook:	#12-16 Orvis 1524 or other 1X heavy, 2X long nymph hook
Thread:	Brown 8/0
Tail:	Two thick brown goose biots
Abdomen:	70 percent fox squirrel and 30 percent Awesome Possum dubbing
Ribbing:	Black Krystal Flash
Wing Case:	Dark gray goose or dark natural turkey
Thorax:	Same as abdomen, pick out dubbing
Head:	Tying thread

Black Stonefly Nymph

Hook:	#12-16 Orvis 1524 or other 1X heavy, 2X long nymph hook
Thread:	Black 8/0
Tail:	Two thick black goose biots
Abdomen:	Blend of black wool and fox squirrel
Ribbing:	Black Krystal Flash
Wing Case:	Dark gray goose or dark natural turkey
Thorax:	Same as abdomen, pick out dubbing
Head:	Tying thread

CHAPTER 5

Terrestrial fishing can challenge your casting skills. You must often present your fly underneath overhanging brush and with a calculated "splat." Too much splat, and you may spook the fish; not enough, and it may not show interest in your offering.

Terrestrials

By midsummer, most of the major hatches have passed. Late summer Tricos remain, but that is a morning game, and the weather has not yet turned cool for fall *Baetis*. The once-abundant underwater food supply has dwindled to tiny nymphs and caddis larvae. Cress bugs and freshwater shrimp become the primary subsurface food supply. Hungry trout now become opportunistic and begin to look for other foods.

Traditionally, most fly fishers packed away their rods, hung their vests, and began to think about next season. Fortunately for us, a group of fly fishermen from Carlisle, Pennsylvania, sought to unlock the summertime secrets of the Letort Spring Run. The Letort was filled with stream-bred brown trout, and any good hatch brought these wary fish to the surface. But once spring lapsed into summer, many of the hatches had passed and many quit fishing.

However, careful observation by a few Letort regulars soon revealed a summertime secret. During the hot and hazy days of summer, these trout seemed to rise for no apparent reason. So Vincent Marinaro and Charlie Fox set out to fool the brown trout of the Letort. Terrestrial fishing became a new phenomenon back in the 1940s, when Joe Brooks published an article stating that terrestrials were a "revolution in fly fishing." The article also featured the tag-team combo of Vincent Marinaro and Charlie Fox. Welcome to the dawn of modern terrestrial fly fishing.

Much has changed since the early days of terrestrial fishing, and other anglers such as Ed Shenk, Ed Koch, and Harrison Steeves III added their names to the terrestrial fraternity. Many new and innovative terrestrial patterns were developed, thanks to

Many consider Vince Marinaro to be the father of modern American terrestrial fishing. A plaque is mounted in his honor near Fox's Meadow on the Letort.

new synthetic materials that hit the fly shops in the early 1980s. These materials were more durable than the quill and deer hair used on the traditional patterns and withstood much punishment. Many books were published on terrestrial fishing, including Ed Koch's *Terrestrial Fishing* in 1990 and *Terrestrials* by Ed Koch and Harrison Steeves III in 1994 (both published by Stackpole Books). Soon patterns like the floating foam Japanese beetle, black foam Sparkle Beetle, and the Steeves Firefly became household names. Terrestrial popularity quickly spread across the state and beyond, and fly-fishing gear found rest much later in the fishing season.

I absolutely love terrestrial fishing. Terrestrial season can be more predictable than trying to plan to fish a particular hatch. On any given day, insects may not hatch, but on most warm summer days, terrestrials will be on the water. Even though terrestrials are a dependable presence on trout streams, fishing can be demanding at times. Terrestrial-feeding trout may become selective not only to a particular insect, but also to size and color. Terrestrials may have to be cast under tight, overhanging trees, bushes, or bridges. On the other hand, terrestrial fishing can sometimes be a cake walk. If trout are on the prowl, they may take any fly that lands with a plop. Even poorly cast flies can entice violent strikes when the trout are willing.

The terrestrial family includes hundreds of land-loving insects. Of these, ants, beetles, crickets, and grasshoppers are the favorites for both trout and fly fishermen. Terrestrials fall to the water's surface by chance. Though these bugs have no interest in the stream, they call the grasses, bushes, and trees surrounding the stream home. With wind, rain, or just bad luck, terrestrials find themselves in the water, and in trouble.

Ants

One early spring, when the winged ants were starting to swarm to make more ant colonies, I was standing in Fox's Meadow on the Letort. As these

Ants most often come in red, black, and red and black. Red ant patterns can be effective, since most anglers fish black patterns.

swarms began to intensify, I stood there watching the water's surface, hoping to find just one trout breaking the glassy surface. The ants soon began flying over the stream, and along came a sudden burst of wind, sending a smorgasbord of helpless ants to the surface. As the ants started to drift downstream, I noticed a rise, followed by another and yet one more. I managed to tie on a fly and land one brown before the rise ended as quickly as it had started.

During the summer, ants become a reliable food source for hungry trout. Ants live everywhere—in trees, soil surrounding the stream, decaying logs, and many more places—and there are lots of them. They come in black, brown, cinnamon, and fiery red. Ants also come in many sizes, from large, black carpenter ants to tiny cinnamon ants. Mating ants have wings and can provide brief, but intense, activity whenever they fall in the water. Because of all the different types of ants, a well-rounded ant selection should include different sizes, colors, and pattern styles.

In addition to color and size, which you often have to match, you should also consider how the pattern floats on the water. At times, trout may want a higher floating pattern or one that is sunken or lying low in the film, and a pattern with the wrong silhouette may go drifting by. If I'm fishing over a rising trout in glassy water, I start off with a foam or deer hair ant imitation. Both the deer hair and the foam flies float low in the surface and have more accurate profiles than a dubbed-body fly. The deer hair fly is realistic and the deer hair has a shine that imitates the natural's shimmer, but it can be difficult to see and not nearly as durable as the foam pattern, which floats well and can take a beating. Dubbed-body ant patterns such as the Fire Ant float well, are fast to tie, and are extremely durable. For many trout, a

reddish ant is a change of pace, because most anglers fish black patterns.

I most commonly fish ants on #14-18 hooks in black and bright orange. To imitate the large carpenter ants, I carry a few black fur or foam patterns in size 12. Don't be afraid to fish larger-than-usual patterns. One day I was having a miserable time on Falling Spring Branch. It was sunny, hot, and crowded. The trout were lying low and hiding out. I wanted to fish my favorite spots, but they were occupied by other anglers, so I went and found a spot that I hadn't really fished before. I

Terrestrials such as ants, beetles, and grasshoppers work on streams across the country, from Pennsylvania spring creeks to Western waters such as Milesnicks Spring Creek near Bozeman, Montana (above). JOHN RANDOLPH PHOTO

To imitate ants, carry fur, foam, and deer hair patterns in a range of sizes from size 12 to 22.

tried just about every terrestrial, terrestrial-dropper combo, and nymph—nothing. I put on a size 12 Chernobyl Ant for kicks and shot it right along a multiflora rosebush; immediately, a sixteen-inch brown gulped that meaty fly.

On the opposite end of the spectrum, ants from size 18 to 24 work well when trout are rising. I start out large and work my way through different colors and smaller sizes until I get a take. I tie these small ants in black, cinnamon, and bright orange and in fur and foam versions. When trout become fussy, I go with a black or orange Deer Hair Ant, which is one of my favorite ant patterns because it floats on the water like a natural. It is hard to spot on the water and fragile, but it is an easy pattern to tie and it always pulls through for me.

Any ant pattern can be difficult to see after it hits the water, and all of these patterns can be modified so that you can see them better. Some flies have built in visibility aids, such as a Parachute Ant, which can be tied with any color of wing post (orange and white are popular) to enable you to see it easily under a variety of lighting conditions. I often modify my basic fur ant (either the black version or the Fire Ant) by adding a tuft of white CDC after I wrap the hackle and before forming the fur head. To make the Deer Hair Ant easier to see, I often secure a short piece of fluorescent-orange

Antron in the middle of the fly after completing the body and trimming the deer hair fibers to create the legs.

If I am casting to a feeding trout, I watch the trout's riseform to help me decide whether I fish a foam, deer hair, or fur pattern. If the trout's nose is clearly breaking the surface, then I try the higher floating fur-bodied ant first; if the trout looks to be pushing water, then I go with a lower floating foam or deer-hair pattern. Whenever I encounter a difficult fish feeding on glassy water, I try a deer-hair ant. What the pattern lacks in durability, it definitely makes up for in effectiveness.

Unlike beetles or grasshoppers, ants don't crash to the surface or splash on the water, so present your ant pattern so that it lands gently on the water and fish it with a dead drift. If your ant pattern is dragging, even slightly, you'll most likely get refusals. An ant may struggle, but it still lacks the strength to swim across the surface unless the water is almost still.

Sinking ant patterns, which can be as simple as regular fur-body or deer-hair patterns fished wet, can be effective at times. Tiers have designed flies specifically for sunken ants with epoxy bodies, which some anglers report good success with. Because sunken ant imitations are so hard to see, I recommend fishing them behind a small indicator fly such as a beetle or parachute mayfly pattern. In fact, an effective method for any ant pattern—sunken or floating—is to fish it on 12 to 16 inches of tippet behind an easier-to-see dry fly.

For the most part, ants are always an option to consider during the summer and are excellent change-up patterns when a fish refuses your first offering. For instance, if you are fishing a mayfly or caddis or even a larger hopper pattern and get a refusal, wait a few moments, let the fish settle down, and then drift an ant by the trout. There are times, however, when fish feed exclusively on ant "hatches."

During late spring and late summer and fall, large numbers of winged males and queens begin to fly in swarms to mate. After mating, the males die and the females drop their wings and set out to find a worthy location to build a home. Unfortunately, it is hard to predict when these swarms will occur. Ants can swarm at any time during the spring, summer, and fall, depending on the species of ant. I have found ant migrations to be common in the mornings on my home waters, but other anglers report that swarms are more prevalent in the afternoons. According to some, flying ants have a propensity to swarm several days after a heavy rain. Whenever it happens, when the ants fall to the water the trout rise with reckless abandon.

Most fly fishers fail to carry winged ants in their boxes, so even if they are on the stream for one of these events, they are unprepared for it. Consider yourself warned. I tie black and cinnamon patterns on #16 to #20 hooks and use white CDC, light dun hen hackle, or synthetic winging material to duplicate the wings. You can always clip off the wings and fish your pattern like a regular ant, so it is better to be safe than sorry.

Black Deer Hair Ant

Hook:	#14-22 Orvis 4641 (1X wide, 1X fine, big eye)
Thread:	Black 8/0
Body:	Black deer hair
Legs:	Deer hair tips

Beetles

I cast beetles to rising trout, or when I hope to bring one up. I fish beetles in the rain and wind, as well as on sunny days. Day in and day out, beetles are my go-to patterns. Why do I love beetles? I think trout can become infatuated with them. Apparently, I'm not the only one. Famed spring creek angler Mike Lawson once wrote in an *American Angler* article: "If I had to pick one dry fly to use on spring-creek waters, without hesitation I would choose a black beetle."

Ants are great, but a box full of beetles can't be beat. Beetles reign supreme in the terrestrial family. They live everywhere, from grassy meadows to rotting logs. Beetles are the first terrestrials to crawl on the stream banks, and they are often the last to be out when the leaves change color and colder weather sets in. A day does not go by from early spring through late fall when trout do not feed on beetles.

There are approximately 24,000 species of beetles, and they come in many shapes, sizes, and colors. I tie beetles in many different sizes and colors

Fire Ant

Hook:	#14-22 Orvis 4641 (1X wide, 1X fine, big eye)
Thread:	Tan 8/0
Body:	Amber Orvis Dry Fly Spectrablend; blend in 30 percent Scintilla Hot Orange for a brighter fire ant
Legs:	Cream or gray hackle to match body

Note: Other body colors can be black, brown, and cinnamon

(with and without rubber or hackle legs) but in only a few general shapes. In *Terrestrials,* Koch and Steeves write: "Most of the beetles we tie will probably be oval or rectangular. These two general shapes have served anglers well for years, and the subtle differences from one beetle to the other do not seem to make much difference to trout, which don't bother to classify too many beetles according to shape." So there you have it: there is only so much you can, or should, do with a beetle imitation. I most often fish black beetles, but one side of my terrestrial box—which I call the "roach motel"—is packed with brown, gray, iridescent, and green beetles from size 12 to 22.

Crowe Beetle

Hook:	#6-22 Orvis 4641 (1X wide, 1X fine, big eye)
Thread:	8/0 black
Overwing:	Black deer hair
Body:	Peacock herl
Head:	Clipped deer hair

Japanese beetles are abundant in the overhanging brush along many spring creeks. Though you can make your beetle patterns as fancy as you like, simple peacock-herl-body patterns work just fine.

Black Foam Beetle

Hook:	#12-16 Orvis 62KC or other curved 1X short, 2X heavy hook
Thread:	Black 8/0
Body:	Peacock herl
Legs:	Black hackle clipped on top
Shell:	Black Fly Foam

Note: You can also tie this pattern with Krystal Flash, hair, or rubber legs, or leave out the legs altogether.

If I'm searching for trout, I generally cast large patterns (#12-14) against stream banks and along exposed weed beds. Willing trout may rise and inhale the fly, and others may show interest but refuse it. If a fish refuses it, I don't move on; I have found a trout willing to play.

I fish a beetle differently, depending on the situation. If I'm searching for trout, I generally cast large patterns (#12-14) against stream banks and along exposed weed beds. Willing trout may rise and inhale the fly, and others may show interest but refuse it. If a fish refuses it, I don't move on; I have found a trout willing to rise. I either size down my imitation or try a completely different pattern. If I encounter rising trout, I try a small (#14-22) first and change color, size, or pattern depending on the fish's reactions. If trout refuse my foam patterns, I go with a #16-20 Crowe Beetle, created by Pennsylvanian John Crowe. This fly often seals the deal when other patterns won't, and though the deer hair is fragile, the Crowe Beetle works well even when torn up.

This brown inhaled a beetle fished along a deep bank. Throughout the summer, beetles are my go-to pattern.

When fishing beetle patterns, don't be too concerned about allowing your pattern to land gently. I like to "splat" the pattern on the water to imitate the natural, which is a dense insect that more often than not hits the surface ungracefully, alerting trout from a long distance. So take everything that you've learned to make a delicate presentation cast, and ignore it. Cast forcefully so that the leader turns over more quickly, sending the beetle imitation to the water. Splatting a beetle can also be a last option for rising trout that has stubbornly refused your other patterns. Instead of calling it quits, try splatting a beetle just short of or off to the side of the fish. I have found that many times the trout turns and attacks the beetle. Be sure that you are just splatting the fly, however, and not your entire fly line.

Grasshoppers and Crickets

Grasshoppers get all the glory. Anglers out West share stories of epic days when the winds were just right and large trout lined up along the banks, gorging on hoppers being blown into the water. The popular method of fishing a dry fly with a nymph dropper is even called "Hopper-Dropper" fishing in some circles, and the grasshopper imitation is a popular choice when a high-floating dry fly is needed.

You seldom hear too many hair-raising cricket stories. But in my experience, crickets catch far more trout than hoppers. I use them as searching patterns to cover the water and when I want to fool a trout that is already rising. On the spring creeks that I fish most often, large trout often come from nowhere to gulp down a well-placed cricket. Anglers around the country have also reported good success with crickets, especially on water that is pounded daily with hopper patterns.

When I was younger, I would occasionally chum up trout by throwing live grasshoppers in the water. After throwing out a few live ones, I would get downstream of the fish, wait for my wakes to settle, and then put the imitation over the fish. Catching

The meadow through which this stream flows is prime hopper habitat. As air temperatures rise and hoppers become more active, many land in the stream.

the grasshoppers was more challenging than the fishing. They have powerful legs that rocket them into the air, and many times a hopper leaps with no clue as to where it intends to land. That is just one of the ways a grasshopper lands in the water. Other times, hoppers try flying across larger spring creeks and lose steam before making it across. This may be why hoppers are effective when fished in the middle of the stream, not just along its edges.

It's time to fish hoppers when you see them leaping away from your invading feet as you walk through grassy meadows, usually around late June in the East. Keep your ears open at night or early in the morning as you watch Trico spinners fall to the water. When you hear crickets chirping, start fishing a cricket imitation. Once hoppers and crickets start to get active, it doesn't take long for the fish to start looking for them. Once trout get a taste for these big, meaty meals, it seems they are hooked and on the hunt along banks, weed beds, and shallow riffles, and generally spread out through the stream. I have also

Hoppers are popular, but crickets often catch more fish. You can modify many of your favorite hopper patterns so they imitate crickets just by using darker materials (dark brown and black).

noticed trout cruising calm areas searching for these meals.

Hoppers and crickets make for outstanding searching patterns. Hoppers are best fished in grassy meadows, but crickets can live anywhere around a spring creek. Cast these leapers tight to brush, at bank edges, and along any weed beds or undercuts. You can even fish them over likely holding areas midstream. I have found that both crickets and hoppers are best fished dead drift, and sometimes a subtle twitch can be effective, especially if the pattern has rubber legs. One technique I like to use when fishing hoppers and crickets is to deliberately cast onto the bank with a slack line and then allow the current to tighten the fly line and pull the chunky meal into the water. Bankside trout are often lurking beneath and quickly snatch up the fly.

My two favorite hopper and cricket patterns come from Ed Shenk. All of Shenk's flies are simple to tie. One day, I was watching Shenk tie a Letort Hopper. As he started carefully trimming the deer hair head, he said, "Now I feel like a barber." True of almost all of Shenk's simple flies, it is his scissors skills that bring life to the patterns. Being able to look at a fly full of deer hair or white wool and

taking a nip here and a nip there is the true art to these proven spring creek patterns.

His Letort Hopper and Letort Cricket have stood the test of time and, in my opinion, need no improving. They float low in the water, and though they are simple, they have the prominent body, wings, and big head of the naturals. Patterns with rubber legs and foam can also work well (especially in broken currents or for suspending a heavier nymph), but I think that sometimes too much material on the fly ruins its profile. On many clear spring creeks, I have found that the simpler the pattern, the more effective it is. Plus, the Shenk patterns are quick to tie, which means I can keep my boxes stocked without a lot of time at the vise. Some of the other grasshopper patterns take me much longer to tie, and I don't think they are any more effective.

Shenk reports in *Fly Rod Trouting* that both he and Ernie Schwiebert independently invented similar patterns to solve similar situations, which is why he often calls his Letort Hopper, the Shenk Hopper. This is testimony to the effectiveness of this style of hopper pattern on the Letort. "Coincidentally, Ernie Schwiebert contrived a terrific hopper pattern also called the Letort Hopper. Ernie's pattern started with a yellow nylon-yarn body, matched but divided mottled turkey-quill wings (like the Joe's Hopper), and a clipped deer-hair head with tips extending to the rear. My pattern started with a pale yellow dubbed spun-fur body and a mottled turkey wing with the feather folded, tied flat, and trimmed in a broad V. The head is naturally tan deer hair, tied and clipped the same way as in Ernie's pattern. So, while I was tying and fishing my Shenk Hopper on the upper Letort and showing it to very few other fishermen, Ernie made a few visits to Charlie Fox's meadow and showed the Schwiebert Hopper to Ross Trimmer and Charlie [Fox]. They promptly named his hopper the Letort Hopper. Everything in these patterns was a series of coincidences, and neither of us knew that our similar patterns had identical names. So

It's time to fish hoppers when you see them leaping away from your invading feet as you walk through grassy meadows, usually around late June in the East.

A Letort Cricket also makes an excellent indicator fly, especially when there is glare on the water.

I've added *Shenk* to my version of the Letort Hopper because I wouldn't want to be accused of pirating Ernie's fly. The Letort Cricket, which came about after the Letort Hopper and other hoppers began to be refused regularly, is my creation."

In addition to the black cricket, I carry several colors of hoppers, including patterns with yellow or orange bodies and tan deer hair wings, and a pattern with a light green body and wing. Though rubber legs can be effective on some patterns, I have not noticed a difference in the pattern's effectiveness with or without them. One disadvantage of the Shenk deer hair patterns is that they can be hard to cast on a windy day. I make do, but you might be better off with a low-profile foam pattern that drives through the wind.

Letort Cricket

Hook:	#8-16 Orvis 1523 (1X fine standard dry fly) or 4641
Thread:	Black 6/0
Body:	Black Fine and Dry
Underwing:	Black dyed goose feather, folded, tied flat, and trimmed in a V shape
Wing:	Black deer hair
Head:	Spun, clipped black deer hair

Letort Hopper

Hook:	#8-16 Orvis 1523 (1X fine standard dry fly) or 4641
Thread:	Yellow 6/0
Body:	Yellow, cream, tan, or orange Fine and Dry
Underwing:	Mottled tan turkey feather, folded, tied flat, and trimmed in a V shape
Wing:	Tan deer hair
Head:	Spun, clipped tan deer hair

CHAPTER 6

Streamers are often a wise choice for targeting a stream's larger specimens. Try dead-drifting them near undercuts and between and around mats of vegetation.

Crustaceans and Baitfish

've saved these two groups for last, but they are the meat and potatoes for a lot of spring creek trout. I've lumped these together in the same chapter primarily because crayfish, cress bugs, and shrimp are all crustaceans, and crayfish seem to belong more in a chapter on streamers than one on crustaceans because of the patterns that imitate them and how they are fished. No matter how you organize them, they are incredibly important trout foods.

Shrimp and Cress Bugs

Trout have the upper hand if you don't have shrimp and cress bug imitations in your box. Not only are they present in spring creeks in large numbers, but they remain active all year and therefore are always available to trout. I have watched trout grab a clump of moss to forage for these succulent crustaceans. Freshwater shrimp and cress bugs are sometimes referred to collectively as scuds, and they are equally important on many tailwater fisheries.

Sow Bugs (Cress Bugs)
Sow bugs live in spring creeks, weed-filled tailwaters, and even some freestone streams—as long as they have necessary vegetation. Because sow bugs live in watercress beds, they are also called cress bugs, and that is what I commonly refer to them as in the text. *Asellus,* the most important species of sow bug, lives across the continent.

Cress bugs range in color from gray to olive. Viewed from the top, they look oval, but their side profile is flat. They have seven pairs of legs that extend out rather than underneath their bodies, which helps keep the flattened appearance. Two pair of antennae protrude from their heads, instead of a single pair like other aquatic insects. Other aquatic insects have three thoracic segments, whereas a cress

A natural sow bug and Ed Shenk's imitation. It's a pretty close match.

bug can have four to forty. Cress bugs can range from 1/4 to 3/4 inches long, and baby cress bugs are just tiny versions of the adults. Cress bugs produce new broods every few months, which is why they are so abundant.

Cress bugs are scavengers that clean the stream by feeding on dead plants and animals. They are found clinging to rocks and aquatic vegetation and also hiding within the soft substrate associated with many spring and limestone spring creeks. Cress bugs are not built for swimming. They prefer to slowly crawl around as they forage. When threatened, a cress bug may roll up into a ball for protection. Cress bugs dislike bright light, so they are more active when the sun is low or on cloudy days. Cress bugs primarily live in those areas of a stream that have vegetation. Where you do find them, there are typically a lot of them. Trout will root through vegetation to feed on them or hold downstream waiting for cress bugs to drift by.

I have come to favor a few patterns to match these tasty meals. For cress bugs or shrimp, I like Ed Shenk's cress bug. The Shenk Cress Bug is trimmed so it takes on an oval, flattened appearance that perfectly imitates the natural. It is quick and easy to tie. The body of the imitation can be dubbed with gray muskrat or a fifty-fifty blend of gray muskrat and brown mink or olive-dyed muskrat.

Another good cress bug imitation is the Ray Charles, invented by Bighorn guide Bob Krumm and reputably named because even a blind person could catch a fish with it. I discovered this simple fly on a trip to the Bighorn, where anglers use it in a wide range of colors including olive, gray, tan, or pink. The body is a few turns of ostrich herl with a pearl flashback top and red thread head.

The Ray Charles is a go-to fly in Montana, but who would have thought of using it back here in the Eastern spring creeks? One day I was fishing Boiling Springs Run, the small spring creek that flows into the Yellow Breeches, and not doing very well. The trout were not happy that the sunshine had brought out such a heavy crowd of fly anglers and were lying low. I tied on a Ray Charles I had left over from the Bighorn after I had tried just about everything else. To my amazement, it caught trout, and it now has its own compartment in my nymphing box.

Adapting the Ray Charles for my home streams taught me an important lesson. There are a lot of great patterns out there, and you can often catch difficult fish by showing them something different than what they are used to seeing. Any pattern developed for tailwaters or spring creeks is worth adding to your collection and just might give you an extra edge.

Shenk Cress Bug

Hook:	#14-18 Orvis 1641 or other 1X short, 2X heavy hook
Thread:	Olive 8/0
Body:	Gray or olive-dyed muskrat

Fishing Cress Bugs and Shrimp

Shrimp and cress bugs remain active all year, so they are constantly found in the bottom drift. I usually try a shrimp or cress bug first, or fish it in tandem with another fly because they are so prevalent in the spring creeks that I fish. During the late fall, winter, and early spring, shrimp and cress bugs become the major underwater food supply when many of the other aquatic insects have hatched for the year. Shrimp patterns also do double duty as caddis, even on freestone rivers.

When shrimp and cress bugs become dislodged from vegetation, they drift with the current until they regain their grip on something. Trout feed on these two underwater crustaceans just as they would on drifting insects, and standard dead-drift nymphing techniques work to represent the dislodged naturals. Keep the imitation as close to the bottom as possible. If I have to add a piece of split

shot, I keep it 10 to 12 inches from the fly to prevent snagging bottom. Plus, some pressured trout will refuse a fly if the split shot is too close to it.

Because shrimp can be almost ubiquitous in many of the spring creeks that I fish, and because I feel confident in my Simple Shrimp's ability to catch trout, I frequently fish a tandem rig with a Simple Shrimp as the first fly, and then I'll attach another fly to 12 to 16 inches of tippet that might represent a midge or any of the insects that may be hatching at the time, such as a small Pheasant Tail to imitate a *Baetis*. Because you can wrap the shank of the Simple Shrimp with weight, plus add a bead, the fly can do a good job of sinking your rig in moderate currents without much split shot. Since I like to fish these flies so that they tumble in the currents along the stream bottom, I'll put on as much split shot as necessary, removing any if I hang up frequently.

This Letort jewel fell for my Simple Shrimp. The fish may not be that large, but they all count—especially on the Letort.

Ray Charles

Hook:	#14-18 Orvis 1641 or other 1X short, 2X heavy hook
Thread:	Red 8/0
Wingcase:	Pearlescent Mylar strip
Legs:	Gray or olive ostrich herl
Head:	Tying thread

Scuds (Freshwater Shrimp)

Scuds, or freshwater shrimp, are much more common and abundant than cress bugs. They thrive in a wide range of spring creeks, tailwaters, and spring-fed ponds. Shrimp populations can become astronomical, reaching numbers by the thousands per square meter. There are many important scuds, but *Gammarus* leads the pack.

Shrimp or scuds are most commonly a transparent olive to yellowish olive color, but some species of *Gammarus* can be tan or gray. When at rest, they are shaped like a crescent moon, which is why so many shrimp patterns are tied on bent hooks. When they swim, they extend their bodies, accounting for many successful patterns that are also tied on straight-shank hooks. Shrimp have prominent blood lines running through their bodies, short stubby tails, and two antennae extending from the head. Seven pairs of legs that hang underneath the body of the shrimp are used for swimming and grasping.

Like cress bugs, shrimp breed several times per year and quickly populate streams. To breed, males grasp the females and swim locked together until mating is completed. Some flies are tied to duplicate the double-stacked mating shrimp, but I have not noticed them to work any better than single shrimp patterns, and they take more time to tie. Even while some shrimp are mating, hundreds upon hundreds of single shrimp are still along the stream's bottom. After mating, the female shrimp carries around a noticeable orange egg sac. Trout may key on these pregnant shrimp, and many patterns have orange in them. I wrap a little bit of orange fur in the middle of my Simple Shrimp to match the egg-carrying female. The young shrimp hatch fully developed but are microscopic imitations of their parents.

When death is imminent, shrimp turn orange. Shrimp can die of natural causes or get caught off guard when streams recede or flows are dramatically cut back. When waters begin to rise, large numbers of orange shrimp can enter the drift. Trout may key on these orange shrimp, so having a few on hand at all times is not a bad idea. I know that on the Bighorn and on the Colorado at Lees Ferry, orange shrimp are very effective.

A natural shrimp (scud) and Heck's Simple Shrimp.

This Big Springs brown took a streamer bottom-bounced like a nymph.

Many times when collecting shrimp in eastern spring creeks, I have found that for every ten olive-colored healthy shrimp, there can be as many as four or five orange-colored shrimp. To match the orange shrimp, I tie my Simple Shrimp with an orange dubbed body.

Like cress bugs, shrimp live on decaying plant and animal matter and are found hiding in the weeds and rocks. Unlike cress bugs, which live in patchy communities, shrimp thrive everywhere throughout a healthy stream, so they are always a wise choice as flies. Because of their wide range and abundance in the spring creeks that I fish, when I rig a tandem setup, one of my patterns is generally a Simple Shrimp.

Shrimp swim by darting five to ten inches at a time and then rest. They straighten out their bodies while moving, but when resting, they curl up and drift with the current. To view this, put a few in a clear cup or fill your palm with some water. Sometimes this movement is to the side, hence their given name of "side-swimmers." Shrimp do not like the light, so they are more active during mornings and evenings and on overcast days.

I match freshwater shrimp with a pattern that I developed called the Simple Shrimp. I designed this pattern back in the 1980s after collecting insects out of Falling Spring. I was amazed to see just how many were clinging to the vegetation and rocks. Stomach pump samplings also showed me just how much these spring creek trout fed on scuds. I wanted to design a pattern that better matched them, and my Simple Shrimp has become a staple fly in my nymphing box. I fish it all year and at all times of the day.

The pattern is tied on a curved hook, which matches the natural's shape when it is drifting in the current. The buggy dubbing fibers move in the current, and the Swiss Straw back imitates the prominent blood line on the shrimp. I tie this fly in olive, yellow-olive, or gray, and will use a bit of orange dubbing to imitate pregnant or dying shrimp. Fly imitations with movement and some

sparkle seemed to take more trout than hard, static imitations. After all, these are live insects that wiggle around. Imitations for both cress bugs and scuds can be tied on hooks ranging from size 14 through size 18. On Western spring creeks, shrimp and cress bug imitations can also be dressed on size 12 hooks to imitate larger scuds and sow bugs.

Simple Shrimp

Hook:	#12-18 Orvis 62KC or other 1X short, 1X heavy up-eye hook
Thread:	Brown 8/0
Back:	Tan Swiss Straw unwrapped and split in half
Rib:	Silver Ultra Wire (small)
Body:	A blend of fifty-fifty olive and light sow bug Spectrablend dubbing

Note: On Eastern streams, I most commonly use #14-18.

Baitfish and Crayfish

When most anglers think of fishing spring creeks, they envision casting small drys to rising trout or perhaps sight-nymphing small midge pupae to fish. But like freestone stream trout, spring creek trout also fill up on crayfish and baitfish, and experienced spring creek anglers aren't afraid to pull out the heavy artillery to catch a stream's larger trout. Sometimes streamers are the only way to lure trout from their hiding places. Many fly fishermen are

Trout use the weeds in a spring creek as cover. Often, these weeds form mats across the surface, and the only way to entice the fish from out under them is to use a streamer.

hesitant to fish streamers, either because they don't know how or because they prefer not to, but streamers catch a lot of fish.

Baitfish and crayfish are essential parts of a trout's diet. Many fly anglers believe only big trout prey on them, and though it is true that larger fish are more piscivorous than small ones, even small trout feed on baitfish. One day when I was fishing the small, weed-choked Falling Spring, I decided to toss around some streamers. I had just returned from smallmouth fishing on the Susquehanna River and

had a box full of poppers and streamers for small-mouth bass. As I pondered over my fly selection, I thought to myself, "Why not toss around that four-inch streamer?"

To an extent, this streamer did look like a fin-gerling rainbow. So I tied it on in hopes of bring-ing out a trout over twenty inches. I worked the undercut banks and deeper runs around the weed beds. I was astonished when I finally hooked one, though it was not the lunker I envisioned. Sur-prisingly, a rainbow no longer than the streamer

Fall browns love streamers. You can tie smaller versions of your favorite streamer for fishing with lighter rods. JACK HANRAHAN PHOTO

attacked the fly. I have landed large trout on streamers, but this proved an important point for me: streamers can be effective for trout of all sizes.

Baitfish patterns can be imitative or designed to elicit aggressive reaction strikes from fish, very much like large spinner baits, which imitate nothing in the stream, are designed to provoke a predatory response in bass. Many articulated or rubber-leg patterns serve this function, as does the venerable

Mickey Finn with its flash body and eye-catching reds and yellows.

I generally steer clear of the attractor patterns except for Woolly Buggers, which don't really fall into that category when they are tied in subdued colors to imitate natural foods such as sculpins, crayfish, and leeches. I prefer more imitative patterns such as the Shenk Sculpin, which looks just like the natural when it is in the water. I think the more natural-looking representations perform better in a clear spring creek, though I'm sure I could be proven wrong. Trout strike garish streamers for many different reasons, and no doubt they can be effective, but day in and day out, I have more confidence in imitative patterns, and I fish patterns more effectively when I have confidence in them.

Most good streamer fishermen have spent a great deal of time observing baitfish in their environment and have adapted their fishing techniques to better imitate the naturals. From my bait-fishing days, I learned that trout don't like to feed on dead minnows. (Something has to be left for cress bugs and crayfish!) Live, healthy minnows they like, and crippled or injured minnows are even better. For this reason, even when I dead drift the pattern, I either make sure that the fly is tied from materials that move in the water on their own (without help from me) or that I twitch the fly every now and then through the drift.

When injured, minnows and trout fry do one of two things. They poke at the surface or bounce on and off the stream's bottom. Both these behaviors can turn on a trout like a light switch. To imitate crippled minnows, you can dead drift your streamer, imparting slight twitches every once in a while. Though the standard strip retrieve works, I have found that dead drifting streamers is much more effective and allows me more precise control to keep the streamer on the bottom and to steer it around the abundant weed beds.

Sculpins and crayfish prefer to lie on the bottom when resting, often around rocks and other structures. Crayfish also hide under rocks, especially when they are spooked. Sculpins and crayfish, bounce up and down off the stream bottom, and when startled do not swim for great distances. Crayfish swim in spurts just like sculpins, but they do it tail first, and just fall headfirst back to the bottom. I have seen both crayfish and sculpins bounce almost horizontally off the bottom, only to move a few inches up or down the stream at one time. Depending on water depth, this bouncing movement can be a foot to several feet up into the current and matched with a technique called "sculpinating." (See page 104 for streamer fishing techniques.)

I like several different streamer patterns. My all-time favorite is the Shenk White Minnow, which has caught trout everywhere in the world. It can imitate many types of minnows including trout fry, which are a reliable food source when these young fish are in the streams. One aspect of the

I carry a few different colors and sizes of streamers in my box, as well as flies that have different actions in the water.

Shenk White Minnow, which I think many anglers overlook in fly design, is its soft texture. When a fish bites down on it, it may hold it for a little longer than it would if the fly were hard. A lot of successful soft plastic bass and saltwater lures have this characteristic as well. Ed Shenk called these soft creations "the flies trout love to chew."

Zonker-style patterns are also very effective, and on my home waters, I most frequently fish Zonkers tied with a gray rabbit-strip wing. Rabbit undulates in the water even when the fly is just drifting along and pulses enticingly when stripped. My Big Eye Rainbow is another favorite, not only because it imitates a common prey item for larger trout—baby rainbow trout—but it has a prominent eye, which I think may trigger a predatory response in some fish. Imitations can be tied on a variety of hook sizes, and I primarily fish size 4 to 10 patterns tied on 2XL streamer hooks. My favorite sculpin pattern is the Shenk Sculpin in black and brown. Muddler Minnows and Whitlock's Near Nuff Sculpins also fit the bill.

Many of the sculpin patterns do double-duty as crayfish patterns, depending on how they are fished, but specialized crayfish patterns that I use include the Claw Dad, Clouser's Crayfish, and Whitlock's Soft-Shell and Near Nuff Crayfish in sizes from 4 to 10. Good crayfish imitations should ride hook point up so they are less likely to snag bottom. Other important components to a high-quality crayfish imitation are movement and materials that keep their shape underwater. Effective patterns are tied with materials that have a lot of built in movement, such as Furry Foam, webby hackle, leather, or rabbit strips.

Shenk White Minnow

Hook:	#4-10 Orvis 8808 or other 4X long, 1X heavy streamer hook
Thread:	White 6/0
Tail:	White marabou
Body:	50/50 blend of white rabbit and white wool-dubbing looped and trimmed to shape
Head:	Tying thread with painted eyes

In the fall, streamers work well for aggressive, prespawn browns and brookies.

Black Shenk Sculpin

Hook: #4-10 Orvis 8808 or other 4X long, 1X heavy streamer hook

Thread: Black 6/0

Tail: Black marabou

Body: Black wool in a dubbing loop, wrapped, and trimmed to shape

Fins: Black deer hair

Head: Black spun deer hair

Big Eye Rainbow

Hook: #2-10 Orvis 8808 or other 4X long, 1X heavy streamer hook

Thread: White 6/0

Body: Round pearl Kreinik Braid

Underbody: Pearl Angel Hair

Overbody: Olive Angel Hair

Side: Red calf tail tied-in sparsely

Head: White thread with painted eyes or adhesive-back 3/16-inch Miracle Eyes

Claw Dad

Hook: #1-6 Orvis 8808 or other 4X long, 1X heavy streamer hook

Thread: 6/0, color to match body

Eyes: Lead dumbbell eyes, 1/30 or 1/20 ounce

Head and Body: Olive, black, or tan chenille

Legs: Black or olive round rubber legs

Claws: Kreel Claws to match body

CHAPTER 7

The bow-and-arrow cast is just one of the many specialized techniques that are useful for fishing in tight quarters. One of the most important techniques is to learn how to stalk trout and cast to them accurately.

Techniques

Fishing Under the Surface

I know this may sound like heresy to some spring-creek purists, but I learned to fly fish by fishing bait with my fly rod. At first I didn't have any books; I just took what I learned with a spinning rod and went from there. The first time I went fishing in a spring creek, I was fishing nymphs, and that method seemed like a natural extension of fishing bait. All those days spent flipping a minnow or red worm paid off. The two types had a lot in common: it was better if you got close to your target, and you had to drift the fly on the bottom, managing the slack line so that you could set the hook when a fish took.

Nymph fishing is very similar to fishing bait with a fly rod. When I first started fishing, I drifted worms along the bottom, working the slower side eddies first before fishing the main current, all the while adjusting the amount of split shot on my line so that the bait bounced along the bottom at the same speed as the current. Like fly fishing, I fished close to the trout, sneaking close to a good riffle or run before I started fishing. Also like fly fishing, I flipped my bait upstream, leading the drift with my rod down and then past me. It wasn't very different from what I do now.

Even if you prefer dry-fly fishing, knowing how to nymph can save the day when weather or stream conditions are tough or there is no surface activity to bring fish up. Whenever I arrive at the stream, I first look on the surface. If there is no ac-tivity, I most often switch to a nymph. Once you determine that you need to fish a nymph, turn over a few rocks or root around in the weeds to see what the most predominant food is, and match it as best you can. Also note the less predominant ones as backup options if your first fly choice doesn't work that well.

Many people think nymphing is difficult, but it really is quite simple once you learn to read the water and detect takes. Most fly fisherman look at the runs, pockets, and riffles as a whole rather than breaking them down into different sections. I first look for and fish the slower edges. That is where you are most likely to find nymph-feeding trout because they do not have to fight the heavier current. I also work behind and in front of rocks and weed beds because they, too, slow down the water. Then I focus on the main channels and runs. Trout can lie just about anywhere in a spring creek, so the better you cover the water, the more you increase your chances of catching fish. The key is to cover the prime lies more thoroughly.

Because the fly is drifting subsurface, the takes are subtle and may go unnoticed. We all miss takes, but it helps if you can watch the trout's reactions to the fly and watch your line for pauses or your strike indicator for any erratic movements. If I detect any pause through the drift, I set the hook. Sometimes it's bottom; other times it's a trout. Experience has taught me to always set the hook at the slightest movement.

You most often cast upstream to stay behind the fish where it can't see you. You want to be almost directly downstream of the fish to minimize the number of currents you have to cast over to eliminate having to mend your line, but you want to be slightly off to the side so that when you cast upstream your line doesn't go over the fish. You must approach the water cautiously because you will be getting close to your target, whether it is an actual trout or just a piece of likely looking water.

You can fish nymphs from a long distance away and right up close. The short game makes it easier for you to cast accurately and set the hook faster, but sometimes you'll have to make a long (over 20 feet) cast upstream and strip in line as the fly drifts back, very similar to what you would do if you were fishing a dry fly. The traditional upstream dead drift is probably the hardest of all three nymphing techniques. With this method, takes can be hard to detect, with or without an indicator. When you notice a take, you must be lightening quick on the hook set. As soon as the line hits the water, begin retrieving the fly line no faster than the current. Retrieving the line too fast pulls the nymph and makes it look unnatural. As you retrieve the line, begin to slowly lift your rod tip by

High-stick nymphing requires a tight line and a raised rod tip to keep as much line off the water as possible.

I wasn't able to catch this brown until I added a second split shot. Make sure to add enough weight to keep your fly ticking bottom and adjust your weight frequently.

raising your wrist slightly. If you have the rod in motion and a trout happens to take the fly, you can set the hook more quickly than if you were just holding the rod.

When I make long casts with nymphs, I stop the rod at two different levels, depending on current speed. If currents are slow to medium in speed, like most spring creeks, I follow straight through with the forward cast, pointing the rod tip right where I want the nymph to land. It is helpful to keep your thumb on top of the rod handle because it helps you aim the fly. I then end the forward cast parallel to the water's surface. The fly may not reach the bottom as quickly as if I had used a conventional tuck cast, but that is not needed in slow to medium currents. If the water is fast moving I will stop the rod high, forcing the fly to tuck

under my leader. This helps drive the fly into the water. You can cause your fly to tuck by fishing a relatively long leader and using a weighted fly (with or without additional split shot). All you have to do is stop the rod abruptly on the forward stroke (at about 10 o'clock) and the momentum of the weight on the leader will cause the rig to tuck under your rod tip.

The method that I much prefer is what many refer to as tight-line nymphing. Tight-line nymph fishing requires short casts of twenty feet or less. Because your casts should be short with this technique, you need only one or two false-casts to get the fly out. After you cast upstream, try to keep the line straight and tight from rod tip to fly. As the drift starts, slowly lift up with your casting hand to raise the rod and take up the slack line as

Indicator Nymphing

I fall somewhere in the middle of the road when it comes to indicator fishing: They are useful and also a hindrance at times. I use them when prospecting likely runs and riffles. The indicator helps me place the leader and line so the fly drifts through the fine edges along the faster current. In many cases, the edges may only be a few inches, so that indicator makes it much easier to hit the sweet spot. On the other hand, I will not use them when I have spotted a trout. If you have spotted a trout, then you should be able to see the take. I also refrain from using indicators while I'm fishing over smooth, glassy slicks. The "plop" of the indicator can startle trout in flats. Some pressured fish actually become conditioned to the sight of indicators and will simply move out of the way as the indicator drifts downstream. In these situations, I just use the end of my fly line as an indicator, or fish an indicator dry fly.

Even though indicators can help you detect strikes, successful nymph fishermen still watch for signs underneath the water to tell them when a fish has taken the fly, such as a white mouth or a flash.

Strike indicators can make it much easier to see the trout take the fly, especially when the indicator obviously pops forward during the drift. But the signs of a take can also be a little more subtle and the indicator may just pause during the drift. I advise beginning anglers to set the hook at anything looking like a trout take.

Though the normal rule for the distance at which to place your indicator from the fly is $1^{1}/_{2}$ times the water depth, I always place them high up on the leader, unless I am using the strike indicator to suspend my fly at a certain depth. I don't like to guess the depth of a pool and then place the indicator just above what I feel the pool depth may be. My reason for this is simple: The surface current is flowing differently than the current down along the bottom. Placing an indicator too close to the fly does not allow the fly to get to the bottom and can also make the nymph drag. Both result in refusals.

Spring creeks are full of food, and most of the time, nymph-feeding trout will move only a few inches to take a dislodged insect that happens to be drifting by. When you are working upstream, it is critical to cover the good water inch by inch. I start by working the most likely areas first. Then I begin working across the area in intervals of five inches by casting upstream. As I'm working across, I watch where the indicator has drifted and just keep working across the area until I have fished it completely.

Indicators come in all shapes, sizes, and colors, and are made from a wide variety of materials ranging from foam, yarn, putty, and even small pieces of floating fly line. Each indicator has pros and cons, so you have to try several to determine what works best for you. Self-adhesive ones are fast and aerodynamic, and I carry some of these in my vest for special situations, but they aren't adjustable and can fall apart. Yarn indicators are good, but I have found that the small ones suitable for spring

Sight nymphing is as exciting as casting dry flies to rising trout. Strike indicators aren't necessary if you can get close to the fish.

creeks get waterlogged after a day of nymphing. I now use Lightning Strike indicators, which are round indicators that use a toothpick to keep them secured to the leader. They come in fluorescent orange and yellow and small (1/4 inch) and large (1/2 inch) sizes. They float high and are adjustable and easy to cast. Some anglers don't use the tooth-pick and instead just thread the leader through the hole in the indicator twice.

In addition to using split shot, you can also fish heavy flies, such as Copper Johns (above) and other beadhead patterns, which sink quickly.

it drifts back to you. The rod is in motion and that helps to set the hook much faster than retrieving the slack line with your line hand.

I most often fish a tight line like this when fishing nymphs upstream. There are more things that can go wrong with a long cast. You can set the hook too late, you may not get the right drift, and you may catch your line in the tree behind you. Though long casts are needed at times, I will always get as close as I can. I like stalking up on trout, whether I can see them or just hoping they are holding in a likely spot. Tight-line nymphing works well for fishing along undercuts and weed beds and in runs and riffles. A high rod tip while you are nymphing with a tight line allows you to keep your line out of all those unwanted currents (little or no fly line should be on the water) and gives you precise control from rod tip to fly, which makes it much easier to detect strikes.

I use a version of the tight-line technique when I fish a spot from an across-stream position. Sometimes this approach is called high-sticking because you are following the drift of the fly with your raised rod tip, generally extending your arm out so that you can get more reach to keep your line off of any tricky currents. Casts with this technique are short, and sometimes just flipping the leader with your rod tip is enough. I let just enough line out past my rod tip so the nymph just reaches the bottom of the stream. Hold the rod high, and lead the drift downstream. The fly should always be behind the rod tip so that it makes it easier for you to detect strikes. Strikes are more noticeable since the line and leader are taut.

Sometimes fishing places like undercuts, working along a stream's edge, and high-sticking require a side approach. In these cases, I stealthily position myself to make the best cast possible. I am not a big fan of mending the fly line during the drift because so many times I have been mending just as a trout took, and I lost the fish. But sometimes you have to mend, so I do one simple line mend just as the line hits the water. On larger streams, I position

myself at about a 45-degree angle and cast across the current. As the line hits the water, I flip my fly line upstream to try to make the fly line perpendicular to the current. Then I simply lead the drift downstream with my rod held over as much of the faster current as possible, always keeping my rod tip pointed at my indicator or at the end of the fly line throughout the drift.

Water currents, depths, and velocities are constantly changing, so be sure to keep adjusting the split shot to keep the nymph in the right area. One split shot can make a big difference. If that fly is drifting too high, trout allow it to pass right over. An excessive amount of weight is productive only in catching all the moss off the rocks. So work with the weight. Don't be lazy, pinch on a split shot, and think you can fish the entire stream with setup. I often adjust my weight several times in one riffle to make sure that I am only ticking bottom occasionally.

Roll casts can be good for dry flies, but they really shine when making repeated casts with a nymph or streamer. Not only do they eliminate all of the false casting that can tangle your split shot or multiple-fly rigs, they don't dry out the flies that you want to sink. In tight quarters where you do not have enough room to make a conventional backcast, the roll cast is indispensable.

To make a roll cast, draw the line back slowly, stopping the rod at your shoulder for casts of less than twenty feet. Go back farther if you're casting longer distances. Wait for it, wait for it, and then when a nice loop (some call this a D loop) forms, make a quick stroke forward, stopping the rod tip high for dry flies or following through a bit more for nymphs and streamers, unless you want them to tuck under the leader.

The essential thing to remember about a roll cast is that the forward stroke is exactly the same as a regular cast. You are only modifying the back stroke. This is important because most beginners tend to sweep the rod tip down toward the water on the forward cast rather than stopping the rod

Nymph Leaders

I use three different nymphing leaders, depending on stream conditions, the width of the stream, and whether I am able to wade. I use a short nymphing leader for smaller spring creeks like the Letort or Falling Spring, which have relatively shallow pools and runs. The short leader will easily get my nymph to the bottom without hindrance to the drift.

On larger spring creeks where I may encounter much deeper water, I use a longer leader to get my fly to the bottom. I also use a long leader on streams where I cannot wade, such as Mossy Creek in Virginia. Although the stream is narrow, I still need a longer leader to eliminate unwanted underwater drag. If it's sunny out and the water is clear, I use a lighter tippet for nymphing. I designed my Clearwater leader to taper to 5X but still turn over nymphs.

In shallow, narrow streams, I use a short nymphing leader. If you approach the fish carefully, you can often get close.

Basic 8¹/₂-foot, 4X Nymphing Leader

.017"	.015"	.013"	.011"	2X	3X	4X
12"	14"	14"	14"	12"	14"	25"

Basic 10-foot, 4X Nymph Leader (Long)

.017"	.015"	.013"	.011"	2X	3X	4X	5X
15"	16"	16"	16"	12"	14"	25"	20" to 26"

5X Clearwater Nymph Leader

.017"	.015"	.013"	.011"	2X	3X	4X	5X
12"	14"	14"	14"	12"	14"	14"	25"

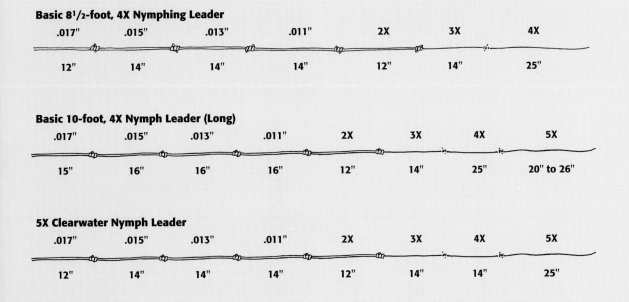

Basic Roll Cast

Start with your rod tip low and the slack out of your line, and begin raising your rod tip.

Keep drawing back on the rod until your rod tip is slightly past vertical and there is a nice D loop behind you. Make sure the rod is angled slightly away from you.

tip high enough so that the line has a chance to unroll toward the target.

Chucking Streamers

When I first started fishing streamers, I would cast across the stream and then just allow the fly to drift and then swing downstream across the current, sometimes twitching the fly line to impart extra motion to the fly. Though I managed to pick up a few fish here and there, I knew there was a better way. Eventually, I began to change the way I fished my streamers, which enabled me to catch the stream-wise trout that I grew up spooking.

On smaller spring creeks, you'll usually be able to see your streamer underwater as you fish it, which helps you adjust your techniques to get the presentation that you want. If the trout are following your fly but ultimately refusing your pattern, you may need to adjust how you are stripping the fly or the size, shape, color, or action of the fly. The best streamer fishermen always adjust their retrieves until they find a combination that works. Be willing to experiment.

Begin your forward cast with the same stroke as the forward cast for your overhead cast. On a good roll cast, you only modify the backcast stroke.

Stop the rod tip high, pointing toward the target. Do not sweep the rod tip down to the water.

Instead of the conventional strip retrieve, I like to bottom-bounce a black Shenk Sculpin, Shenk White Minnow, or Woolly Bugger along under-cuts and weed beds to imitate sculpins, crayfish, and injured minnows. Depending on water depth and current speed, I add split shot or soft weight to the leader about two inches from the streamer, so that when the shot hits the bottom, the fly just tickles the stream bottom. After you cast, allow the streamer to sink to the bottom and then lift the rod tip a few inches to raise the streamer off the bottom. As the fly drops back, repeat the lift. I have

moved hundreds of trout by using this technique, which my friend Ed Shenk calls "sculpinating."

Shenk describes the technique in his book *Fly Rod Trouting* (Stackpole Books) for fishing the Shenk Sculpin, which he sometimes refers to as "Old Ugly": "One of my favorite methods, and proba-bly the most deadly, is to cast the Shenk Sculpin upstream, allow it to sink to the bottom, then bounce it downstream in short and long hops, al-ways keeping the fly fairly close to the bottom. The fly darts up from the bottom and then de-scends again. When I slack off the line to allow the descent, I try to maintain contact with the fly so that any 'take' will be transmitted up the line. This is such an unusual presentation that the large trout really fall for it."

I have watched Shenk work his magic with a great deal of effectiveness. One day I had just pulled into Bonnybrook on the Letort and began to put on my hip boots. Two anglers were swinging their streamers under the bridge. As they left, Ed appeared from downstream and he continued upstream to the bridge. He gave me a welcoming wave, but I felt as if I was intruding on him. So, I started to walk upstream, but he called me back. I was surprised to see Ed try fishing under the bridge since two anglers just went through there, but I kept my mouth shut.

Ed had on one of his white minnows, and with a flick of his wrist, he cast the fly so that it landed right at the corner of the bridge. Ed slacked up on the line, letting the fly drift back under the bridge. Then he made an upstream line mend and began stripping in the line with a slow retrieve, letting the line settle back downstream after every twitch. I watched and learned. With another twitch, the line went tight, and Ed raised back on his little 6-foot rod and pulled out a small brown trout. As I looked on with a smile, he said, "It is all in how you fish them."

In *Fly Rod Trouting,* Shenk also describes a technique for fishing over silty bottoms that at first sounds like it's more appropriate for enticing bonefish on a South Florida flat. "A variation of this retrieve [sculpinating] is preferably done in an area with a silt or marl bottom. In this presentation, the off-the-bottom twitch is very slight, so the fly makes only a feeble move but shoots up a small, visible puff of mud. This can fool even the most cautious trout." Perhaps the mud is a trigger for fish

Working streamers through the weed mats is one of my favorite tactics for big spring creek trout.

Fishing a Shenk Sculpin or Shenk White Minnow is often an effective way to cover the water of some larger pools.

used to hunting their prey, be it sculpin or crayfish, over these types of bottoms.

In addition to sculpinating your streamers, you can also fish them dead-drift like you would nymphs. By high-sticking, you can work a streamer along the likely areas such as undercut banks, weed beds, and sunken debris and just let it drift in the current. Sometimes you can add a gentle twitch for a little more movement. If you make longer casts, you'll have to mend line downstream of the drifting fly as soon as the streamer hits the water so that when you twitch the fly it continues to drift and

swim broadside to fish. Most pressured trout are used to seeing the same old stripped streamer, but when they spot something drifting in the current as if it were crippled, they often grab it.

When fish want a more active retrieve, I'll work the streamer across stream with short strips. Once I move into position above and across from the fish, I cast the fly far enough upstream so that it can settle to the bottom. I follow the swing with the rod tip while stripping in line to bring the fly to life, keeping the strips under two inches. I'll also fish this method when searching undercuts for big

Downstream Mend for Swimming Streamers

Cast across stream.

Begin raising your rod tip.

Flip the line downstream.

As the loop forms, move your rod downstream.

(continued on page 110)

Once the line lands on the water with a downstream belly, start your retrieve.

trout. The key with streamer fishing is to be flexible enough to try a combination of dead drifting and enticing strips to see what the fish prefer.

If you want to match an injured minnow nudging the stream surface, try a minnow pattern such as a Shenk White Minnow and add just enough split shot so the fly will drop a few inches below the surface. With a tight line, twitch the rod tip so the streamer rises to the surface. This can be repeated over and over, and works especially well for covering weed beds. Often trout are hiding within the dense weeds and just waiting for something to float by, and when using this technique, you can twitch and drift your fly with precision through any gaps in the weeds, or above or below them.

Sometimes, the only way that you can get your fly back into deep undercuts and under log jams and other structures is to feed your fly downstream to where you suspect the fish is holding. Before you cast, make sure that you have a lot of slack line to feed into the drift. With this technique you don't often have to cast that far at all. Simply flop your fly out in front of you, and as the fly drifts downstream, strip more line from your reel and feed it into the drift. You can also fish a dry fly in this manner. This is a deadly small-stream technique that few people use.

After the fly is downstream of you, you can fish it back upstream, which sometimes does the trick. Point and lower the rod tip right at the streamer to help it stay down in the current. Next, with short two-inch strips of the fly line, begin to retrieve the streamer. Strip, pause for a moment, and strip again. You can combine techniques by stripping your streamer upstream in this manner as soon as it swings below you.

Many times a big trout may become interested in your streamer and come out of hiding to take a peek at it, but ultimately refuse to eat the fly. In these cases, I try two tricks to keep their attention. If I see a trout coming for my stripped fly but then start backing off, I may slack up on the streamer so that it starts to drift right back to the fish. Sometimes the fish eats; other times it heads home. The second technique that I'll try is to tease it and make it mad. As the trout reaches the streamer, I pull it from him, stopping the streamer about a foot or two away. If the fish doesn't charge the fly, I'll cast again, and sometimes the fish will take it then. If the trout charges and nails the fly, be careful on the hook set. I have left many streamers in the jaws of a trout that took voraciously.

Though spring creek trout are normally sensitive to tippet diameter, you can, and should, use a heavier tippet diameter when stripping streamers for trout. Not only does the heavier tippet protect you against savage takes, but it also makes it easier to cast the larger, heavier fly. I favor streamer leaders tapered to a tippet of 3X or heavier. If I just happen to be fishing nymphs with a 4X leader, I will just nip off the 4X, leaving the 3X for my streamer. If I am tossing streamers all day I'll fish a leader that reflects the conditions. For sunny skies and clear water, I fish 3X (and maybe even 4X); if the water is stained or skies are cloudy, I choose a 2X tippet. I like to keep my streamer leaders around eight to nine feet long. My favorite streamer leader formula is 12 inches of .017-inch-diameter monofilament, 18 inches of .015 inch, 18 inches of .013 inch, 18 inches of .011 inch, and 32 inches of 2X. If I want to fish a streamer leader that tapers to 3X, I modify this formula to include 15 inches of 2X and 24 inches of 3X.

When fishing nymphs or streamers, cast wide loops to avoid tangling your line or hitting yourself.

Basic Upstream Mends

You can use this essential mend to sink your nymphs or streamer or get longer drifts with a dry fly. While this sequence was shot on placid water, you would use this mend if there was a fast current between you and your fly. Cast across stream.

Raise your rod tip and begin to lift the line off the water and flip it upstream.

Allow time for the belly to form.

Drop your rod tip. The belly in the line buys your flies more time to sink before drag sets in. You can repeat this basic mend through the drift of the fly if you are fishing in faster currents.

Dry Flies

I fished nymphs most of my early years because I found it easier to catch fish with subsurface imitations. I soon started trying more dry-fly fishing, which was frustrating, but I kept working at it. Rising trout often lie just a few inches below the water's glassy surface. Many times, I spooked these trout before the line ever reached the water. If I was lucky enough to get a cast to fall without spooking a rising trout, my fly pattern was often refused. Then there were the times the fly would drag as soon as it fell to the water. Other times, the leader would not roll over correctly and my fly would land in a tangle of tippet. Many anglers say nymph fishing is more work, but I feel dry-fly fishing is just as hard, only you are snagging trees and bushes instead of bottom.

Getting the perfect dry-fly drift requires several things to all come together. Start by building a good leader with a tippet that complements the dry fly. Make a cast so that the leader collapses the way it should. Finally, approach a trout in a way that minimizes that amount of currents that can

When fishing dry flies on calm currents, you need to use a long leader with a fine tippet. Make sure that you do not have too much slack in your line so that you can set the hook quickly.

Charlie Meck hooked up during a Trico spinnerfall. To be able to see your fly, you need to first know where to look, which means learning how to cast accurately so you can anticipate where your fly is going to land.

foil your drag-free drift. Similar to nymph fishing, you can fish dry flies from any position (upstream, downstream, or across stream), but your position can have a lot to do with your success. One of the main goals when fishing a dry fly is to keep the fly line and leader out of as many complicating currents as possible. The more currents you eliminate between you and the fish, the better your chances of preventing drag.

A properly built leader allows the dry fly to drift without drag. If the tippet is too short, the fly will drag. If the fly is bulky and the tippet goes unchecked, the leader may not form S curves, and your fly will drag. If the tippet is too long for the fly, then it may be hard to roll the tippet over. I make a few practice casts before fishing so I know I have the right leader and tippet for the fly I am fishing. If I do not see nice curves through the leader when it lands on the water, then I modify it so that it is right. While fishing, I may change the flies several times. This shortens the tippet. So when I notice my fly starting to drag, more than likely I need to lengthen that tippet.

When fishing dry flies, fly and leader need to be accompanied by a well-executed dry-fly cast that collapses the leader. As the line and leader fall to the water, S curves are formed in the leader, which are essential for a drag-free drift. The water surface has lots of different currents, some that you can see, and others you cannot. As the dry fly drifts, the S curves begin to straighten out and allow the fly to keep drifting without dragging. A dry fly would not be able to drift drag-free without these S curves.

A good dry-fly cast is all about getting the leader to break down in midair, float gently to the water, and allow the dry fly to float drag-free. You need to remove the energy from the fly line before it reaches the water by stopping the rod high on the forward cast (about 10 o'clock) and then lowering the rod. The sudden stop combined with lowering your rod tip is what makes a well-designed leader work and allow the fly to drift free of drag. The amount a properly built leader collapses depends on the acceleration of your rod during the forward cast, how fast and abruptly you stop, and the extent you drop the rod tip after the stop.

Though distance casting is rarely important on small spring creeks, it is important to know how to make a range of casts to be able to deal with the many obstacles and obstructions. Some spring creeks flow through thickets of trees that hang in a low canopy over the stream. High grasses and bushes often loom behind you. Weed beds are a constant battle. Following are some basic casts that will get you started, but you should work on your practical casting skills by spending time with a

An upstream presentation is often the best way to fish to trout feeding along a bank. If you were to cast across stream to bank sippers, the faster currents between you and the fly could drag the line. JACK HANRAHAN PHOTO

Floating Your Flies

Most of the gel and liquid floatants on the market work well, but some can't be used on flies tied with CDC or snowshoe rabbit hair. Frog's Fanny, a powdered desiccant-type floatant, has a funny name, but it works very well on all dry flies, including those tied with CDC or snowshoe rabbit fur. Before you fish the fly, brush a generous amount of the powder on the wing of the fly, or any other portion that you want to float. After you catch a fish on your fly, thoroughly rinse all the slime from the feathers, press the fibers between a cloth or piece of chamois, and then reapply the powder.

Frog's Fanny can also be used to fish nymphs. If you want to add a neat visual effect to your nymph pattern, try brushing on a little Frog's Fanny. Once submerged, the nymph will start to collect bubbles around the fly. This can be effective for fishing caddis pupae and emerging mayfly nymphs.

To pretreat my flies before a fishing trip, especially my dry caddis and stonefly imitations, I brush on a little water sealant like Thompson's Water Seal onto the fly with a kids' watercolor brush once I have finished tying it and let it dry overnight. These pretreated flies float like corks and skate high as they swing across the stream. I store water sealant in a glass baby food jar and use as needed. Several companies make products specifically for pretreating dry flies.

qualified instructor and putting your skills to test on the water.

The basic upstream cast is the presentation that makes the most sense on a small spring creek, most of the time. Because you are approaching the fish from below, you reduce the chance of spooking it with your waves and any silt that you kick up by walking on the stream bottom doesn't disturb the trout you will be casting to. Since fish feed facing into the current, this approach is generally the safest way to avoid the chance that the fish will spot you. You will need to make across-stream and downstream dry-fly presentations, but the upstream cast will be your bread and butter.

The first thing to do is to get into proper position to make the cast. The more currents your line and leader travel across, the more your fly may drag, so move to where you are casting upstream across as few varying currents as possible. If the pool is all one placid current, then you have more options, but generally you want to try and get below and slightly off to the side of the fish, so that you can cast your line, leader, and fly in the same current. Because you are probably standing in the same currents as you are fishing, you don't need too many S curves in your leader. The fewer S curves, the easier it is to take up all the slack when you strike, but a skilled angler who learns to strip in line while simultaneously lifting on the rod can successfully hook a fish with a pile of tippet next to his fly.

To put curves in your tippet, come forward on your final delivery stroke with the rod aimed at or slightly above eye level and stop your arm abruptly, as if it were hitting a wall. Many beginning casters never learn how to come to a complete stop on the forward cast. Instead, they follow through which robs the cast of energy, causes wider loops, and can often direct the line down toward the water. If you stop dead cold and slightly overpower the forward cast, the energy from the cast will cause the rod tip to bounce, putting S curves in your leader.

With some practice, you'll be able to adjust the amount of S curves by how hard you stop. If you check the cast by pushing down on the cork handle

The cross-chest cast is good for situations where you want to direct the line away from an obstacle behind your regular casting arm. This cast is not very good for distance, but works well in close quarters. JACK HANRAHAN PHOTO

Cast over and let your line land on weed beds or rocks for a longer drag-free drift.

with your thumb and lifting up on your back two fingers when you stop, you can get even more S curves. I learned this technique from watching Joe Humphreys. Do not check the cast so hard that the line and leader snap backward. After the stop, I drop the rod by dropping my forearm and elbow straight down until my elbow is close to waist level. If done correctly, the line, leader, and tippet roll over with S curves in the tippet.

Before casting, always look behind you for obstacles that could catch your line. Though your casts will tend to be more accurate if you keep your eyes trained on your target, sometimes it makes a lot of sense to watch your backcast, especially if you are casting in tight quarters where an accurate backcast is as, if not more, important than your forward cast. If there are obstacles behind you, a roll cast or a cross-chest cast usually solves the problem. For a cross-chest cast, instead of bringing the rod straight back over the same shoulder as your casting side, bring the rod across your chest, stopping just before touching your opposite shoulder so your backcast goes to the side of the obstacle behind you. Stop the forward stroke at about the middle of your body. If you bring the forward stroke all the way across your body and stop the stroke in front of your casting arm, your cast won't be accurate. The cast will be thrown too far to the side, not hitting the intended area or sighted target. Remember Lefty Kreh's rule: The line goes in the direction the rod tip stops. A cross-chest cast may take some time getting used to, but the time spent is worth it.

If you can't move into a better position, you need to find a way to foil all those back eddies and other tricky currents. Before I learned how to

Cross-Chest Cast

Begin with the rod tip low to the water with no slack in the line. Raise the rod tip gradually and smoothly.

Continue drawing line from the water, being patient not to begin your backcast until the line is off the water (but the leader is still on the water).

Sweep your rod hand back a short distance, coming to an abrupt stop and forming the loop.

Let the backcast unroll.

(continued on page 122)

Cross-Chest Cast (continued from page 121)

Begin your forward cast before the line finishes unrolling all the way.

Continue bringing the rod forward, looking at your target.

Stop the rod in the direction of your target.

As the line unrolls, drop your rod hand.

This brown trout ate an ant pattern fished on 7X tippet. A soft graphite or bamboo rod protects delicate tippets and many prefer them for light-line fishing. JACK HANRAHAN PHOTO

properly make a pile cast, I got a lot of drag when casting into swirling currents that went every which way. Sure, my fly may have landed in the right place, but by the time the trout was interested in it, the fly was skating away like a missile.

Accuracy is the toughest part of the pile cast. The casting stroke remains the same as a regular overhead cast. Aim the fly in the direction of the target, but with an elevated trajectory. Then stop the forward stroke abruptly while keeping the rod tip high. This forward pause followed with a hard check shocks the leader, and the tippet will fall on itself as it settles to the water. As the line settles to the water, quickly drop the rod tip so that it is parallel to the water's surface. Done properly, the leader will "pile" on itself and give the dry fly enough time to drift drag-free. By adjusting the

tippet length, angle of your forward cast, and how hard you stop, you can vary the amount that your leader piles up.

Unlike the stack cast, which is also designed to solve similar drag problems, this cast has the advantage of not requiring a low backcast. Though a stack cast may be more accurate, you need to come back low on your backcast to enable the high trajectory of the forward cast. This cast requires a gentle forward cast, and after you stop the rod, you lower the rod tip to the water. On many spring creeks, a low backcast snags streamside grass and other debris, so I usually choose to make a pile cast.

Weedy spring creeks create their own class of casting challenges. Although you can usually position yourself to cast in weed-free lanes, sometimes that is impossible, and you have to cast creatively. Whether approaching from the side or casting upstream, if you cast the fly over and on top of a weed bed, your fly line won't drift downstream, buying you a longer drag-free drift. If a trout inhales the dry, strike hard to get the line out of the weeds and fully embed the hook. In addition to using weeds in this manner, you can also cast over logs and rocks that are in the stream.

Dry-Fly Leaders

Most of us can detect when our fly is waking unnaturally across the current, but trout can detect even more subtle movements in the fly and leader that we may not be able to see. These subtle movements are often called micro-drag, which basically means any drag on your leader that you can't see but the fish can. To beat this hidden drag, you have to build a leader that has enough slack in it when it lands on the water so the currents don't move the fly unnaturally. Dry-fly leaders must be built to conform to the fly being cast. A dense fly, like a hopper or beetle, straightens out the leader if the tippet has become too short. Take time to lengthen the tippet if that is the case. Be sure the leader is performing just right. The first two casts are always your best chances of fooling a rising fish.

George Harvey designed the leader formula that is the base of most leaders today. His formula has a butt section that comprises approximately 60 percent of the leader. This butt tapers to a midsection and then a tippet. The first four sections of the leader are made from a stiff monofilament, followed by the "hinge" made from soft monofilament. The rest of the leader down to the tippet is also made from soft monofilament.

The Harvey leader formula applies to both dry-fly and nymphing leaders. Some dry-fly leaders can become long when dealing with a 7X tippet. I change the length of the segments to get the leader to perform the way I want it to under certain situations. Harvey also changed the leader to get the results he desired.

Harvey later changed his leader formula, and now uses all soft monofilament from butt to tippet. I still prefer the original style because I think the stiff monofilament helps roll the leader over much better. The original Harvey leader has the first four sections made from hard monofilament. It is getting harder and harder to find, but Mason Hard monofilament works best. I believe Harvey used Dupont first. The "hinge" is always 2X soft leader. From the hinge, the leader is all soft monofilament tapered down to the desired tippet size.

Harvey's revised leader formula, as printed in the September 2001 issue of *Fly Fisherman,* is composed entirely of soft monofilament: 18 to 19 inches of .015-inch-diameter monofilament, 18 to 19 inches of .013, 18 to 19 inches of .011, 18 to 19 inches of .009, 15 inches of 3X, 15 inches of 4X, 36 inches of 5X.

For the record, here is how Harvey describes making the slack-line cast that works well for his leader design. He makes it clear in the article that this cast is not intended for long range targets and that he generally does not cast over 35 feet. With an 11' 6" leader, and an 8 1/2-foot rod, you are already more than halfway there.

"With the shorter line, you can get a better slack leader. With the thumb on the top of the front end of the handle . . . the backcast is made with little arm action but a fast snap of the wrist, so that the line goes straight back and about 9 or 10 feet above the water. As the line straightens out before it starts to fall, make the forward cast with fast wrist action, so the line will straighten out 5 or 6 feet above the water. Follow the line down to the water with the rod tip. . . . Raise the rod tip slowly as the line drifts back. If you raise it up too fast it will straighten out the leader."

If am fishing smaller flies (#18 and smaller), which require a finer tippet to get a drag-free drift, I use a leader tapered to 7X. I'll also go down to 7X for tippet-shy trout, even when fishing small hopper and cricket patterns. Fishing a large fly on such light tippet presents its own set of casting

(Leader Head) Harvey Leader (Original)

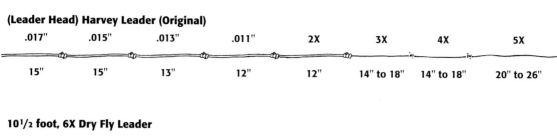

.017"	.015"	.013"	.011"	2X	3X	4X	5X
15"	15"	13"	12"	12"	14" to 18"	14" to 18"	20" to 26"

10½ foot, 6X Dry Fly Leader

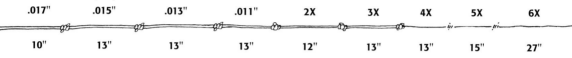

.017"	.015"	.013"	.011"	2X	3X	4X	5X	6X
10"	13"	13"	13"	12"	13"	13"	15"	27"

11'2", 7X Dry Fly Leader (Small Flies)

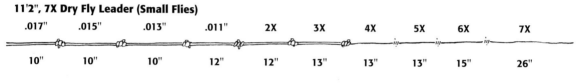

.017"	.015"	.013"	.011"	2X	3X	4X	5X	6X	7X
10"	10"	10"	12"	12"	13"	13"	13"	15"	26"

RICK TAKAHASHI ILLUSTRATIONS

challenges and you must be very careful not to snap the fly off of the tippet, either when casting or setting the hook on a fish.

There are lots of knots from which to choose, but a few simple ones have consistently worked well for me over the years. When tied properly, they have held under tension, and tying them has become automatic, primarily because they are so simple.

I use only four knots for trout fishing, and they have worked well for me. Besides, my fingers have become accustomed to these knots and probably would go on strike if I tried something new. Tests may show that there are other, stronger knots, but I have landed thousands of fish on these simple knots. For tying tippet to the eye of the fly or securing tippet to the bend of a fly for a dropper, I use a regular old seven-turn clinch knot. This simple knot works well, and I would rather be fishing than fixing monofilament to my fly pattern. The clinch knot will usually pull free with any fewer than seven turns.

For attaching leader to fly line, I use a tube nail knot tied with a tube. When I need a loop to connect leader butt to a looped fly line or to loop-to-

loop two sections of tippet, I use a perfection loop. I use a blood knot to connect sections of monofilament when I build leaders or add tippet to leaders. Some complain that this knot is too hard to tie, but it comes easier with practice. If the blood knot is too hard or your fingers like another knot, many fly anglers have informed me that the surgeon's knot is easier to tie.

A knot is only good and strong if it is tied properly. Monofilament becomes weak if it gets too hot, so always moisten the knot with a little saliva before pulling it tight. If you see pigtails on the end of your tippet instead of a fly, you may have tied or seated the knot incorrectly in your haste to get fishing. Take your time.

We have ten fingers for many reasons, but not for knot tying. Learning which fingers to use is essential for tying good knots. When off the stream, practice your knot tying with inexpensive monofilament. Stay away from using your expensive leader materials for your practice, and buy a large spool of the four-pound monofilament that is used on spinning reels. You might also consider purchasing a little waterproof pocket knot-tying guide to refresh your memory while you are onstream.

Combo Meals

For many years, I fished with only one fly. If the trout did not want my dry fly, or the second, or possibly the third, there would be another day. Times have changed. I now like the idea of having two options and often attach a dropper to some dry flies when conditions warrant. I call these "combo meals." This dry fly and dropper combination, or tandem nymphs, can be extremely effective. Anglers have found all sorts of ways to tie multiple flies to the leader, but I think the most tangle-free and simplest method is to tie the second fly off the bend of the first with a clinch or other knot (for many different ways of tying tandem rigs, read Charles Meck's *Fishing Tandem Flies,* Headwater Books).

I'll fish a dry and dropper during the transition times of the year when the water is still too cold for many fish to be on the surface grab. Early in the year, the water is still cold, and few weed beds remain. Even when black stoneflies and early Blue-Winged Olives hatch, trout are sometime hesitant to break the surface. When this occurs, I'll fish a dry to imitate the hatching insect (hoping to find a willing riser) and drop a nymph or emerger off of the bend. If nothing is hatching, I tie on a shrimp or cress bug.

I'll also use a dry fly and dropper when I want help detecting strikes but I don't want to use a strike indicator, or I am certain that a strike indicator will put the fish down. At these times, a dry fly used as an indicator is a wise choice, because it not only spooks fewer fish, but it also provides another

A red San Juan Worm is an excellent pattern to fish as one of the flies in a multiple-fly rig. Many think that this fly doesn't match anything, but there are lots of aquatic worms in many rivers.

A dry fly and a dropper is an excellent rig when you are unsure of where in the water column the fish are feeding.

opportunity for me to hook fish. Sometimes you may want to fish two dry flies, especially if you need a little help tracking a small midge or Trico. Many anglers will fish the small midge or Trico dry 12 to 16 inches behind a larger (but still small) fly such as a Parachute Blue-Winged Olive or beetle. Combo meals also are effective when you are not sure which stage of insect or even what particular insect the fish are feeding on. By fishing two flies, you can give them two different choices. If there is a hatch going on, I tie on a nymph that best matches the hatch. I also use a dry fly and dropper to suspend a nymph over a submerged weed bed, which is a common occurrence on spring creeks. An indicator generally spooks fish in these circumstances while a subtle dry fly doesn't.

In addition to fishing a dry fly and a nymph, you can also fish multiple nymphs, either underneath a strike indicator or a large and buoyant dry fly. Like with dry flies, I tie my first nymph, which is usually a shrimp or cress bug, to the tippet with a clinch knot. Then, with a clinch knot, I secure 12 inches of tippet to the bend of the lead fly, and tie another nymph onto that.

The tippet that I secure to the bend of the first hook is the same size diameter or smaller than the tippet used to connect the first fly. Since I'll often fish a small fly at the end, a smaller diameter tippet makes sense. Plus, a smaller size tippet has the added advantage of almost always breaking before the tippet attached to my first fly if I get the rig snagged on something. This means that you'll only lose one fly instead of two if you have to pull your flies off a submerged log or rock, or out of a nearby tree.

I choose my second fly based on a variety of factors. If there is no apparent insect activity, I generally fish an attractor nymph such as a San Juan Worm off of the lead fly. Some say to tie the "attractor" type nymph first, but I have found no difference. Since I know that I'm going to fish a cress

Most of the time, I fish a Simple Shrimp as the first fly in a two-fly rig.

bug or a shrimp anyway, it's much easier to just change the last fly in the rig. If there is a hatch, or I suspect trout are feeding on a specific insect, I might fish a more realistic fly as the second pattern. One word of caution: When landing trout, always be alert for the other fly in your tandem rig. Not only can it tangle in your net, but it often finds your flesh if you are not careful.

CHAPTER 8

Learning how to spot and creep up on fish is one of the most important spring creek tactics you can learn. Don't think like a trout to catch them; think like a predator.

Thinking Like a Predator

When I was young, I spent most of the time watching trout spook before I even attempted to make a cast. I became frustrated with my lack of success, so I started to learn more about trout in order to catch them. I learned to recognize feeding, sheltering, and prime lies. I started collecting insects, which enabled me to tie more appropriate fly patterns. This newfound knowledge enabled me to catch and release a few small, uneducated trout. Still, the larger trout remained out of my league until I realized what I was doing wrong.

I used to believe you must think like a trout before you can catch one. To some extent, that is true, but there is much more to the story. Of course, it is in your best interest to know what insects trout feed on and where to find trout feeding on these insects. But if you cannot approach a wild trout without spooking it, how will you ever be able to hook one? Even though most of us are not hunting to eat, fly fishers are predators. Anglers must first spot, cautiously approach, and then try to catch a trout—the same basic steps the great blue heron goes through every day in order to survive.

Observing how predators blend into the environment can teach us to dress to match the natural surroundings we are about to enter. Watching predators stealthily move around should show us we simply should not quickly walk up to the stream's edge. Observing how a heron remains motionless for minutes shows us we cannot begin flinging flies as soon as we approach a feeding trout. Instead, we should wait until the trout feels secure. Mimicking the appearance, abilities, and patience of predators will make for fewer trout spooking for cover and more tight lines.

The first of many things I noticed was the way the heron was camouflaged. Although the heron is gray, the dull feathers never reflected sunlight. Though the heron never matched the green meadow grass identically, its overall dull appearance blended perfectly with shadows and dark places around the stream's edge, and from a trout's viewpoint, herons match the sky, making them virtually invisible.

The main lesson to take away from this is to wear clothing that somewhat resembles the stream environment and blends in with the trees, bushes, and lush grasses associated with a trout's habitat. You do not need to match the stream environment exactly. Clothing should not be light or bright in color. Colors such as green, blue, brown, and dull gray blend in well with most stream surroundings and though they might make poor images for books or fly-fishing magazines, definitely spook fewer trout. Wild trout quickly notice white or brightly colored clothing moving around in a lush meadow of green grasses or a rhododendron-choked mountain stream. Choose clothing that is appropriate to your surroundings. In the East, khaki vests are generally a no-no, but they are perfect for blending in with the streamside rocks of the Rocky Mountain West.

Wear clothing that somewhat resembles the stream environment and blends in with the trees, bushes, and lush grasses associated with a trout's habitat. JOE TREGASKES PHOTO

Proper wader color is also important. Trout have extraordinary peripheral vision, and wading puts us right in their domain. Wear waders that closely resemble the stream's bottom or surrounding vegetation, and you'll spook fewer fish. Whether they are chest highs or hip boots, I wear waders in olive, dull green, and brown.

Do not overlook all those gadgets dangling off vest and chest packs. Shiny forceps, zingers, and nippers can send flashes of sunlight into the eyes of wary trout. You can purchase these useful gadgets with nonglare finishes to help eliminate unwanted glare. Put your wristwatch in a pocket or turn the face toward your body. Trout will dart like small torpedoes if the reflection from the watch hits the water in the right spot.

Wild trout become comfortable with many things, but you are not one of them. Trout, over time, have learned that no harm will come from a flock of ducks feeding in the water or from a herd of grazing cattle. In fact, trout can learn to associate ducks and cattle with feeding opportunities because of the vast quantity of insects these animals stir up. Whatever your physique, it is a large and unusual presence to wild trout. Keeping a low profile in and around the stream is paramount. I try to decrease my height by crawling or stooping within twenty feet of the stream to shorten my tall silhouette and make it harder for the trout to spot me. If at all possible, I try to put some cover between the trout and me by using any tall grass and shrubby bushes to obscure my silhouette and hide most of my movement while I cast. By the way, when casting be conscious that your rod tip waving through the air (as well as the line and any water spraying off your fly) can spook fish. Cast to the side of the fish, and whenever possible, use few false-casts.

Many of my clients have poor approach skills and would catch more fish if they worked on stealth. I try to impress upon my clients that we are intruding on the trout; they know the stream better than we do, and they know exactly what should and should not be there. Unless fish have become accustomed to extreme fishing pressure, trout are likely to dart away if they hear or see a human suddenly walking up to them. Great blue herons slowly and cautiously stalk up and through the stream. Their skinny legs never push any water ahead of them, even in the slowest of pools. When a heron finds a good feeding position, it remains motionless until the prey calms and settles.

The angle of your approach depends on many factors such as whether you are working upstream or down to begin with, whether certain structures or other things limit your casting from one angle, and the methods that you feel most comfortable using. You may have a lot of confidence in a downstream drifted dry fly, and chances are that

Whenever possible and practical, kneel. You will spook fewer fish.

confidence offsets the fact that you are more exposed to the trout. All things being equal, and if you have a choice, I generally recommend that my clients stalk a trout by approaching them from downstream.

Stalking a trout from behind puts you in exactly the same current the trout is working and makes it easier to get a drag-free float. The fish can't see you, and the downstream currents mask your approach. If an approach from downstream of the fish isn't possible, try an approach from the side so that you are across from and slightly downstream of the fish.

An approach from straight above puts you in the trout's line of sight. Remember to move slowly when you are working along the stream edge. Spring creeks have lots of deep undercut banks, and although a trout may not see you, it can still feel the movement from the ground above.

Despite taking precautions, you'll still spook a lot of trout when you are wading. There are just too many trout hiding places for you to pay attention to. Because I know I will spook fish when I wade, I try to wade straight along one side of the stream and reach across the stream with my rod to

If at all possible, try to put some cover between you and the trout. Try using the tall grass and shrubby bushes to break down your silhouette. Cover also hides most of your movement while you cast.

Stalking a trout from downstream, you are less likely to alert it.

get over all those unwanted currents or weed beds. Try working the stream with your shadow over the bank instead of out across the water. And if possible, keep your shadow at your side or behind you. This can be difficult because that means that you will sometimes have to fish into the sun. If that is the case, carefully consider your choices for approaching the fish, weighing the pros and cons of each.

Wading

Wading, like all those gadgets hanging off our vests, is a tool and a skill, but anglers rarely pay attention to it. You should wade only when absolutely necessary because trout can often sense when you enter the water. However, sometimes wading is necessary to get into a position that will provide you with the chance to get the best possi-

ble drift over a fish. Moving a foot or two can be the deciding factor in a good presentation.

Cautious anglers never think they are totally safe, even if they have fished the same stream for years. Streambeds can change, and rocks can become slick with algae and weeds. The banks of spring creeks are often undercut and can be unstable. So be careful when you walk right beside a spring creek. Slippery grassy banks can put you in the drink. Muskrat holes can appear from nowhere. Streamside vegetation, like overhanging grasses and aquatic weed beds, can look safe but may be deeper than you think or have soft bottoms. It's best not to step in these weed beds at all, but if you absolutely have to, probe ahead with a long stick or wading staff. When fishing in the winter, the soles of your boots turn into ice, especially if you are wearing felt soles, and that can put you right into the chilly waters. Taking

Pay attention when wading, whether approaching a trout or crossing to the other side. Many spring creeks are silty. Some of this silt can be described as muck. You'll smell it once you reach a certain point, and that point isn't where you want to be.

a bath in a cool spring creek can be inviting on a hot, humid summer day, but it becomes a nightmare any other time of the year.

Many spring creeks are silty. Some of this silt can be described as muck. You'll smell it once you reach a certain point, and that point isn't where you want to be. My best advice is to check silty areas first. Slowly ease one foot into the silt and gently apply weight to that foot. See how quickly it settles into the silt. You can also probe the bottom with a wading staff to determine how soft the bottom is before you take that first step. If the silt

starts to feel solid; step in with the second foot. The same applies with the second foot. Now all your weight is standing in the silt. If you feel yourself sinking, get out by leaning back as you draw out one foot at a time. If you are close to the bank, put your rod down. Lean against the bank and push up with your hands or arms to gain leverage.

Try not to wade in and through the fragile weed beds. Wading into a weed bed tears out and kills the weeds, which are essential to the health of the creek. Weed beds are home to insects, and they hold and keep trout safe from predators. Most weed beds like elodea and watercress grow only in silty areas. I wade around weed beds by wading up along them in the main channels or currents.

When fishing smaller, silty spring creeks, such as the Letort, any silt you disturb flows downstream, possibly ruining the fishing for downstream anglers. When I see someone on a small spring creek, I either fish a different meadow or, on crowded days, give the downstream angler about four hundred yards of water before I get in. If I see that the downstream angler is working upstream, I may even jump in below him. I walk downstream past him, get in about three hundred yards or more away, and then start to fish upstream. When walking downstream, I do not walk right along the bank. Keep a good distance of fifty yards off the stream's edge as you walk down and pass.

For the most part, spring creeks rely on the reproduction of wild trout. Rainbows spawn in the spring, and brown and brook trout spawn in the fall. I tell my clients that spawning trout are off limits! We need the trout to do their thing so we have trout for the future. Trout spawn only in suitable gravel in riffles or shallow-flowing runs, depending on the species. My philosophy is simple. If the spring creek is silty and any disturbance of the silt will harm the redds, I stay out of the stream. If the stream is gravely, then I am less concerned about silt and instead just give each redd a wide berth. I carefully get into the stream about fifty feet upstream of any redds and make sure that I'm not stirring up any silt.

Most of the water that you wade in a spring creek will not be the fast and sometimes raging torrents of a freestone river, but many larger streams have deeper, faster currents. On these streams, scout the area for a better place to cross rather than through the fastest, deepest water. Tailouts are always a good bet. If you have to cross in fast water, slow down and put one foot after the other. Make sure you plant your first foot before taking the next step. Don't try to wade straight across a swift stream, especially when it is deeper

than waist high. Instead, wade in a bit upstream of your target area, and then cross at a slight downstream angle. Going with the current helps you plant your feet and improves your balance.

If you can fish with someone, use the buddy system to help you wade through any water that you do not feel safe in. Spring creeks can be extremely cold, and that cold can stiffen your legs,

When wading be mindful that you may be stirring up silt, which flows downstream and may possibly ruin someone else's fishing.

especially if you have circulation problems. In the buddy system, the strongest wader stands on the upstream side of the weaker partner to shield the weaker angler from strong currents. Can't get your partner out of bed for a morning fish? Invest in a wading staff. A staff is like a third leg and can actually serve two purposes. As you move around, a staff gives you much more balance because you have a solid support to lean on. A staff can also be used as a probe to poke at the streambed for underwater obstacles or sudden drop-offs you may not be able to see. The telescopic wading staff is probably the most popular because it can be stored in a pocket. Telescopic staffs work well on most streams, but in deep pockets and faster streams, I use a one-piece staff (an old ski pole) that can take on my full load if I slip, whereas a collapsible staff may come apart.

Instead of splashing in right up to the tops of your chest waders, fish the water nearest you first. Trout love to hug the bank on many streams, and many trout are caught right along the bank. Tromping around or sending wakes of water through a pool puts trout down. Trout may not see you, but they can *sense* you through vibrations. Wading too close to fish generally sends them scurrying for cover unless they are accustomed to wading pressure. By baby-stepping and shuffling, you slow down and make less of a wake in the water, which means you are less likely to spook trout. If you see a trout starting to drift around, drop to the bottom, or do anything different than what it was doing when you first started approaching it, it is probably sensing your presence. Stop, wait until it settles down or resumes feeding, and then begin to get into position.

Learn to recognize redds (above) and give them a wide berth when you wade.

Baby-stepping is easy to do and does not require any fancy equipment. Instead of taking a full step, try taking just half of one. Be sure to plant your lead foot firmly, and slowly take half a step forward with your other foot. If that does not cut down on water wake, try an even smaller step the next time. Baby-stepping works because it cuts down on the leg and foot movement and significantly decreases water wake and noise. Baby-stepping also increases wading stability.

Many times we just wade too fast, which causes needless accidents and blown opportunities to catch fish. When we wade quickly, we don't take the necessary time to survey the water. Next thing you know, there goes a fish or two. When I first started fly fishing, I had to train myself to slow down, and I eventually began using the step-and-look technique, which is my favorite way to fish, in or out of a stream. After a step, stop and look for rises or underwater flashes as you work your way into casting position. Because you are observing the fish's behavior, you make better decisions about patterns and presentations. If you don't have a specific target, this approach essentially makes you fish more water, and at the end of the day, you'll usually catch more fish— because fish can be where you don't expect them.

Fishy Places

Trout hold and feed in other places in the stream besides the pools, deep runs, riffles, and glassy flats that anglers commonly target. In fact, the hardest places to get a fly usually hold the largest trout, so it pays to try to master the technical presentations required to reach fish hiding in these places. Most anglers pass by these fishy spots because they are not easy to fish. Many of the streams that I fished regularly when I was younger had a lot of fishing pressure, and I often had to share the stream with other fly fishermen. I passed up the riffles and easier runs to learn how to fish the hard-to-reach areas because I knew that they were some of the least-pressured waters in the stream.

This fish was tucked right against the near bank. Fortunately, I knew he was there (I had spooked him in the past), and I cast to him before rushing on to fish the deeper, and more attractive, water on the far bank.

Along these same lines, most anglers tend to fish a particular pool or run from the same side, either because that is the side that provides the best drift, there are too many bushes or other casting obstructions on the other side, or it's the side that everybody fishes from, so it must be the best. Though it doesn't always make a difference, one way that you can get a leg up on the other anglers is to try and approach the pool or run from a different angle. It may just be that the way

Though fish feed throughout a spring creek, certain spots are more attractive than others, and you should focus your efforts there. Bridges (above) and other structures, broken water, edges, undercuts, and weed beds are all prime spots.

the currents help swim your fly from the opposite side provides a drift that the fish haven't yet grown accustomed to. It's worth a shot, anyway.

On the Edge

Trout need adequate cover and an ample food source. If a place in a stream can provide both, trout are sure to find it. Sometimes, however, they forsake cover for food and venture into shallow water. If there is enough water to cover a trout's back, they will be there. I have watched many trout feeding along the edge, even with a dorsal

fin out of the water. Though fish can be spooky in these shallows, they are there to eat. A good presentation with a terrestrial or "match the hatch" fly often entices a quick turn and strike.

The better a food supply, the better the odds that trout have migrated out of the deeper holes and riffles to find a stream's edge, but edge-feeding trout are not just a late spring through summer event. It took a few years before I began spending more time fishing stream edges earlier in the year. Even without the presence of the major hatching insects, I have found trout lying along the edge at any time of the year, even during the winter. Exposed rocks, stumps, dense brush, and fallen trees in and along a stream bank provide more than adequate trout cover, but they also absorb the sunlight, which in turn heats up the branches or rocks. Also, the shallow water in the margins typically heats up faster than the main current. During the winter, midges can be hatching and then need a place to stay warm. Immediately, the tiny midges head right to these warm areas. As they congregate, they begin to attract trout. I have, on many occasions, come upon trout lying directly under these wintertime swarms just waiting for midges to fall to the water.

Even during the winter, midges hatch almost every day on Spring Creek, near State College, Pennsylvania. Every time I make my annual Thanksgiving trip and walk over the wooden bridge at Benner Spring, midges huddle along the warm sides of the bridge. The trackless snow tells me no one has been fishing. Along the bank is a long run of dense, overhanging brush. Within the brush are hundreds of midges, dipping at the water's glassy surface. And just about every time, lying beneath the midges in only inches of water and tight to the bank, is a midge-sipping trout.

But I didn't learn to pay attention to edges winter midge fishing. I learned to focus on the margins of a stream during the summer when ants, beetles, hoppers, and crickets become abundant, and trout often feed on them tucked tight to the bank, sometimes in water so shallow that their dorsal fins are tickling the surface. While terrestrials can get blown onto the water in midstream, ants and beetles frequently forage along bankside vegetation, and tall grasses along a streambank are home to crickets and grasshoppers.

To catch the largest trout, you need to be willing to take a few chances and make a few risky casts.

Wade carefully and watch for sipping rises along banks. Many times these bank feeders go unnoticed by most anglers, but when you find one, it can be a sucker for a beetle or ant. JACK HANRAHAN PHOTO

Emerging insects such as stoneflies can also make trout swim to the edges. When a significant number of stoneflies are crawling to the bank to emerge, trout follow and feed on the nymphs. Black caddis crawl to the edge, just like stoneflies. Grannom caddis emerge by drifting, but they head right to any bankside vegetation to rest. As they congregate, the trout move right in. I have seen this happen on many streams, but nothing like on the Little Juniata River and Spruce Creek. Here, the trout instinctively head right to the bank to feed on the caddis clinging to the trees and other surrounding vegetation.

My favorite way to fish to bank feeders is to stalk them, just like you would deer or other game animals. Good hunters walk carefully and approach slowly. When I hunt for whitetails with my muzzle-loader, I always take a few steps—through leaves crumbling under my weight or through snow—and then scope the woods to look for my intended target. I use the same step-and-look technique when I stalk fish. As I creep along, I look for rises to betray trout feeding on the surface or the white winks and flashes under the water from a trout feeding on nymphs.

I generally approach bank feeders from downstream. The easiest cast to make is from the same side of the stream as your target, but you can cast across stream to a fish feeding on the other side. Because the currents next to the bank are most likely moving slower than the midstream currents, a reach cast is often the best way to beat drag. When making a reach cast, you reach upstream with your rod tip after the stop, which places the fly line upstream of the fly and buys you more time for a drag-free float. A good reach cast is gentle. Though you can make the cast without shooting line, if you feed slack line into the cast as you reach upstream you will not run the risk of straightening your line when you make the reach.

Prospecting is another great way to work the edges. Using the same step-and-look approach, cast your flies along the edge. On many small streams, I keep my cast under twenty feet and rely on a sneaky approach to get close to the fish. With larger waters, my cast may be longer. Nymphs can be presented in the same fashion if a trout is noticeably feeding beneath the surface. Trying to cast a weighted nymph, or weight on the leader, so that it lands softly is the challenge when nymph fishing. I usually move into a position where I'm behind but at an angle to the trout, and I cast far enough upstream of the fish so that hopefully it doesn't spook from the disturbance of the nymph hitting the water. You can reduce the amount of split shot that you would usually use and cast ever farther upstream, which keeps the splash away from the trout and also gives the nymph time to sink. Many

Exposed rocks, stumps, dense brush, and fallen trees in and along a stream bank provide more than adequate trout cover, but they also absorb the sunlight, which in turn heats up the water.

times, this is the only way to fish nymphs on the placid flats associated with spring creek water.

Many times I'll try to trick bank feeders without entering the water. One way that you can do this is to cast straight upstream along the bank. If you know how to throw a little bit of a curve into your cast, you can actually kick the fly tight to the

When ants, beetles, hoppers, and crickets become abundant, trout can be found tucked tight to any stream bank, their dorsal fins tickling the surface of the water.

upstream bank while your line and leader drift off to the side. The other way that I fool bank feeders without getting into the water is to creep up to the stream and just extend my rod out over the bank. I then sort of swing my fly (if it's weighted) upstream of the trout and, with a tight line, allow the nymph to settle to the bottom and drift past the trout. With a dry fly, you can flip out your leader with a quick little cast or use the bow-and-arrow cast to flip your fly to the water.

Though anglers accomplished at making the bow-and-arrow cast can achieve some remarkable distances, this technique really shines for just flicking your fly out on the water with a minimum of false-casting that could spook fish. Here's how you do it. Since this cast is for short distances, you only want to cast your leader. There is a way of casting farther, but it is hard. Grasp the hook bend between your thumb and forefinger, making sure the hook point is outside of your fingers. Trap the fly line against your rod with your rod hand. Pull back on the fly, putting a bend in the rod like a bow. Aim the rod tip at your target. Let go of the fly. Practice this cast before getting to the stream, and I think you'll find that it becomes a useful technique for you. (See photo on page 196.)

When fishing tight to the banks, you'll inevitably have to deal with eddies, which are places in the stream where the current swirls opposite of the main current. These places are extremely tricky to get a good drag-free float, so make sure that you use a good slack-line cast with a long tippet. Another tricky aspect of fishing eddies is that fish may be facing downstream to feed, because the current is actually traveling upstream. If this is the case, it may mean that the fish can see you if you are approaching from downstream.

Undercuts

Trout feeding in the open are challenging enough to catch—you must select the right fly, make a cast that doesn't spook the fish, get a good drift, and then fight and land it. However, many times

Tucked under a bank, trout can avoid predator birds and animals and elude fishing pressure throughout the season. Trout also use undercuts as feeding stations to prey on unsuspecting fish or helplessly drifting insects.

to consistently catch fish on a spring creek, you have to go after the trout where it feels the safest—hidden in undercuts. This type of fishing presents a whole new set of challenges, from the tricky logistics of getting your fly in front of the fish in such a difficult-to-reach place to fighting the fish on its home turf, where it often has the upper hand and has an uncanny ability to find the nearest snag to break off your 5X tippet. Under-cut banks require anglers to lure a trout out four feet or more, and you need patience and a will-ingness to take chances with your casting, even if

that means a break-off or two. To fish these kinds of places requires not only a special set of casting skills, but also a certain amount of patience and willingness to rerig after snagging your fly.

Streambanks, overhanging grasses, bushes, and trees all provide overhead cover for trout to avoid predator birds, animals, and anglers throughout the season. Trout also use undercuts as feeding stations to prey on unsuspecting fish or helplessly drifting insects. Some undercuts are permanent; others are created by the seasonal growth of weed beds and lush meadow grasses on spring creeks.

Undercuts (above) provide cover and protection for trout.

Most trout live in permanent undercuts, such as scoured-out banks or root-balls from neighboring trees, that are formed over time as the stream's current erodes the bank. Roots from overhead grasses, bushes, and trees prevent the remaining soil from falling into the cavern and give trout an excellent place to hide through the seasons. Through time, surrounding trees also provide trout with a place of security. As trees grow, their roots need to grow. Roots grow for various reasons, one of which is that the roots are searching for water. Instinctively, roots head right into the stream. As more and more roots invade the stream, resisting currents begin to flow underneath the massive root-balls, in turn making a nice undercut.

In the spring, warming water temperatures promote the germination of aquatic plants. Roots from within the substrate begin to grow up through the stream. Stretches of stream that were barren gravel flats during winter now flourish with life. Beds of aquatic vegetation immediately play host to many underwater inhabitants. The cress beds quickly fill the stream channel, and the struggle for supremacy is on. As the flowing water and cress beds fight, the water begins to cut paths through the dense weed beds. Trout now move from overcrowded wintertime lies to find food and shelter waiting for them. From these beds, trout can dart out and feed on unsuspecting fish or simply stay hidden and pick off any of the many different insects clinging to the watercress. As spring lapses into summer, another undercut is in the making. Grasses grow high in the meadows, and before long, these tall grasses give way, bending over the stream and providing trout with yet another safe place to hide and feed.

Fishing streamers is a great way to fish these areas of cover, because you can present them from all directions and if working them from upstream, you can actually feed slack into your drift to get the streamer back under a deep undercut. Because they also provide a substantial target for trout, even if you do not get way back under the bank, a streamer might present itself as a large enough food source to the trout to entice it out from hiding. Large predatory fish hunt in low light conditions, and these are excellent times to work a streamer along banks and under overhanging brush.

Whether you are fishing dry flies, nymphs, or streamers, you should have a plan about how you are going to land the fish before you cast to it. Make sure you are using tippet appropriate to the job, and it's worth breaking off some fish to learn about how much maximum pressure you can exert before you break a fish. Using maximum pressure and pulling at right angles to the fish's head will help you turn it out and away from the undercut. Steady pulls are usually not what break the line, it's the sudden jerks. One skill you'll have to learn onstream is when to apply steady pressure and when to back off the fish.

Working Weed Beds

Weed beds are a vital part of every healthy trout stream. Every underwater inhabitant uses vegetation in some way. The insects cling to leaves and sticks, and small fish hide in the weed beds and

Weed-choked runs are hard to fish, but the results are worth the effort.

hope they don't become dinner themselves. Larger trout are drawn to weed beds because they provide shelter and a constant food source, all in one place. Most fly fishermen would sooner pass by weed-choked runs to focus on the easier-to-fish pools, pockets, and riffles, which is good for those of us who learn how to fish them.

Dense mats of weeds are a characteristic feature of spring creeks, and learning how to fish them successfully is part of every seasoned spring creek angler's training. In the spring, watercress, elodea, and duckweed grow in the fertile water, and during some years, parts of a stream can be completely choked with surface weeds, leaving only two feet or less to make a cast. Fly fishermen in the West are faced with similar problems. The larger river bottoms are entirely covered with weeds and algae, which sometimes grow to within inches of the surface.

Though dry-fly fishing is easier than nymph fishing on small, weed-choked streams, it still has its challenges. For starters, any knots on your leader collect weeds and algae, so it is best to use a knotless tapered leader in a weedy creek. As I've mentioned before, the weeds swaying in the currents can create their own microcurrents on the surface of the water, compounding an already difficult drag-free float. Use long tippets. Any weeds that are on your fly can ruin the presentation, so be extra mindful to check your fly frequently. This may seem like a no-brainer, but I've watched many anglers cast and cast a dry fly with a small piece of weed on it without bothering to remove it.

When you are dry-fly fishing, think of the weed beds as structure, which they are, and even though fish may not be visible, always consider the possibility that they are tucked in under the weeds, waiting for something enticing to drift by. Work

This rainbow fell for a scud fished skillfully through a maze of weeds.

the edges of the weeds thoroughly in addition to any of the main channels. As I mentioned earlier in the book, you can cast your fly line right over the weed bed to fish the water in front of, or to the side of, the weeds to get a longer drag-free drift.

Dry-fly fishing isn't much of a problem, but for the inexperienced, fishing nymphs can be a nightmare. At first glance, weed beds look like a maze of bewildering line-snagging entanglements. We know trout are down there because of the many underwater critters weed beds draw in, but how do you get a fly down there? And if you do get a drift and catch a fish, can anything be done to keep trout from ducking into weed beds and breaking the line?

Nymphs present an entirely different set of challenges when fishing in weedy areas. If you become good at fishing nymphs through the weeds you have the upper hand on most other anglers who usually just fish dry flies because it is too much trouble to get a good underwater drift. I don't fish any weedless flies, but I do find that by controlling the amount of weight on my fly, and constantly adjusting it, I can usually get clean drifts. Casting accuracy is also important. By making short casts and fishing a tight line you stand a better chance of controlling the drift of your fly.

Another technique that I use to drift my fly over weed beds is to fish a dry and dropper, or what I call a combo meal. In this instance, I do not use my dry fly as a strike indicator; instead, I use it to suspend my nymph over the weeds. Even if the weeds grow to within 6 inches of the water's surface, you can set your nymph or emerger 4 to 6 inches behind your dry fly so that it drifts over the weeds unimpeded. When I am fishing around weeds, some of my favorite nymphs to use imitate shrimp and cress bugs, perhaps the most predominant food in the vegetation on the spring creeks that I most often fish. Trout often hold just downstream of the weed beds to feed on cress bugs and shrimp. If you are fishing upstream, fish the downstream side of the bed, then both of the side edges.

I fish my streamers much like nymphs, casting upstream tight to the weed beds and letting it drift with the current. Occasionally, I quickly strip in two or three inches to add action to the fly. Highsticking streamers can also be effective. Approach the weed beds from the side and flip your streamer upstream. As it drifts along the bottom, twitch your rod tip up and down no more than an inch. Another way of fishing streamers is to stand above the area of interest, cast down and across, then swing your fly to the edges of the weed beds, and slowly retrieve the fly back to you.

Like when fishing undercuts, once you hook a fish, you need to steer it away from the weeds. As soon as it tries to duck into cover, fight the fish with side pressure. When the fish clears the weeds, keep the rod high until the trout makes another run. When the trout shows signs of being played out, get it to hand and off the hook quickly. Make sure your hands or net are wet before they touch the trout to prevent taking off the protective coating on the skin.

Fishing Bridges

Low-lying bridges are a part of the spring creek experience, and day in and day out they are dependable spots for me to find fish. Bridges provide overhead protection from predators, shade during the day, and a dependable place to find food. Bridges, like other structures, also provide protection for other stream inhabitants. Many baitfish and crayfish scurry under bridges and think they are safe. Many land bugs such as ants, beetles, and spiders can all reside around bridges. These curious insects constantly move about, and one wrong move means they fall into the drink. Underwater insects cling to the pilings, where they find refuge from sun, wind, and birds. For instance, adult caddis and stoneflies often use bridges to elude the sunlight. Bridges absorb the sun's rays and become warm during cooler days, so adult mayflies and midges warm up their cold bodies with the heat from bridges.

Low-lying bridges are part of the Eastern spring creek experience, and the water under them is always a good spot to cover with a fly.

Approach and a good cast are the trickiest parts of the bridge game. If the bridge sits high above the water, I approach from downstream and cast my flies upstream and under the bridge. I prefer this approach because it provides more chances than a downstream approach. With a downstream approach, you must retrieve your fly line back upstream to make another cast. Doing this a few times often puts the trout down. With an upstream approach, you simply let your leader drift downstream and well away from the fish before you pick it up to make another cast.

To cast under a bridge, or under any other structure such as overhanging limbs, you'll be better off with a sidearm cast rather than a standard overhead cast. In a sidearm cast, the rod travels back and forth parallel to the water, and with practice you can unroll the line just a foot or two above the water's surface. Make a few false-casts to get the angle right and make sure you are casting low, tight loops, and then stop the rod in the direction you want the fly to go, driving the line, leader, and fly up under the bridge. Most anglers who are first learning to make this cast, wave their casting arm forward and back too much, casting wide loops. When they make the final presentation cast, they also tend to swing the rod tip around in a wide arc, way past where they want the fly to end up. Remember to stop your rod tip where you want the fly to go. If you are fishing weighted flies with this technique, or weight on the leader, this sidearm cast tends to throw a curve in your tippet, so you have to learn to adjust for that.

Sometimes, however, a downstream approach works best, such as if the bridge is too low for even your best sidearm cast, or if you are upstream of a riser and don't think that you have the time to reposition yourself. You may also encounter a tough situation where you don't have enough room to make even a sidearm cast. If that is case, you can try stripping off a lot of line from your reel and allowing the current to take the line and fly downstream and under the bridge.

When presenting a fly downstream, try not to get in the water unless it is absolutely necessary. Wading stirs up dirt and silt that flows downstream, possibly alerting trout of your presence and spoiling your approach. If you must get in the water, do not move once you get into position. Wait until the stream clears and the trout resumes feeding (if it was feeding). To prevent drag with a downstream presentation, you need to feed your fly line into the drift faster than the flow of the stream so that it doesn't drag.

Here's one way that I do it: Strip a good bunch of line off your reel. False-cast over the bridge, and when you have enough line to get three-quarters the way under the bridge, stop the forward cast. As

If you need to fish under a low lying bridge, tree, or other structure, sometimes a downstream presentation is the only way to go.

Pile Cast (Indicator Variation)

Cast above the bridge and check the rod by stopping your forward cast with the rod tip high. The line bounces back, landing on the water with slack in the line and your leader.

Lower your rod tip as the line drifts downstream. Notice there is plenty of slack line to feed into the drift.

Continue feeding line, extending the drift under the bridge.

the line slowly begins to fall to the water, pull your rod back so the fly drops right at the edge of the bridge and begins drifting under the bridge. If you need to let out any extra line, lower the rod tip to the stream, strip off more line, and allow the current to pull the slack line downstream, helping the line out with gentle up and down motions with your rod tip. If I need to make another cast, I slowly pull my line back upstream. This may startle the fish, so I wait a few minutes before making another downstream cast.

How do you know what to tie on? If trout are rising, then the dry-fly game is on. If there is a hatch, then match it; if it is summer, consider a terrestrial pattern. A well-presented cricket or hopper will entice bridge trout into striking. Not only do ants and beetles fall into the water and drift under bridges, but they also find the crevices in bridges to be suitable homes, and many fall into the water.

If trout aren't rising, I'll often fish a streamer such as a Shenk White Minnow. Because you don't have to worry about drag, streamers are really versatile flies. You can cast the fly upstream, allow it to settle to the bottom, and then strip it back. You can also fish them on a downstream swing by casting across to the opposite bank and allowing the streamer to sink to the bottom, either letting it swing across the stream steadily or gently stripping the fly with two-inch strips, slacking up on the line after each strip, until the swing has ended. I often get strikes as the fly dead drifts back downstream.

Nymphs can also be fished upstream or downstream. The upstream approach is probably more widely used because detecting strikes is easier.

Adjust the weight so the nymph drifts dead drift where you want it in the water column (usually on the bottom). I seldom fish a nymph downstream under a bridge; I would rather toss a streamer. But if you want to fish a nymph downstream, you can attach your nymph to a dry fly as a combo meal or use a strike indicator to help you detect takes. If you are roll casting an indicator rig under a bridge, use a small foam bobber or self-sticking foam indicators, which are less dense, not as bulky, and easier to roll cast under a bridge than large yearn or bobber indicators.

If the bridge is low, a high hook set can pull the fly out of the water and snag the bridge, or if you hook a fish, the leader can catch the bridge and possibly fray, which reduces your chances of landing the fish. I prefer to use a slightly elevated side set by raising the rod with a slight back-and-upward motion. If you can get more line off the water, you will have less water friction to contend with, which means a quicker hook set.

You can also set the hook with a strip strike, which is favored by saltwater anglers. I am not that proficient at strip striking. I'm always striking on

The cover of darkness, or at least low light, is one of the best times to stalk trout. JACK HANRAHAN PHOTO

When playing a fish under a bridge, keep your rod low and to the side. You will prevent your line and leader from scraping the bridge and will apply side pressure to the fish.

Friday when the trout took on Thursday. But practice makes perfect. When strip-striking, you have to be very quick. Water resistance slows down the sharpness of the strip strike. The trout may seem to be hooked well but easily throws the fly when the fight starts because the hook never really embedded into the trout's mouth.

No matter how you set the hook, the trout will probably not want to leave the safety of the bridge. Keep the trout unbalanced with side pressure and try to roll the fish across the current to tire it quickly and give you the leverage to pull it out from under the bridge. I pay close attention to my line and leader while playing the trout. If the line or leader starts flirting with the bottom of the bridge, I lower my rod sideways to drop the line or leader back to a safe level. Once the fish is out from under the bridge, get the rod up in the air and bring the trout to hand.

CHAPTER 9

Spring creeks are special, shared resources. We must protect these treasures for future generations. The author peeks inside Hagn's Letort Log to see who was fishing there lately.

Spring Creek Conservation

Some spring creeks, such as Falling Spring Branch, are vibrant with life. As you walk the banks, hoppers, beetles, and ants scurry away from your feet. Red-tailed hawks hover over the meadows, looking for mice or other unlucky prey. Kingfishers and great blue herons cautiously work the stream for a meal. Duckweed, elodea, and watercress gently sway in the cold currents, providing home to abundant insects. Trout, insects, and birds all share the stream in perfect harmony. Many of the meadows have native green willows and sycamores to provide cover and shade for birds and trout. Falling Spring is tiny—only four to fifteen feet wide through most of its length—and flows through lush meadows, some of which have become backyards. Despite human encroachment, the stream is still teeming with insects and trout. Unfortunately, other spring creeks are in need of some help.

Some spring creeks have banks barren of lush grasses and bushes because years of livestock overgrazing destroyed the stream banks. With no vegetation to hold the soil in place, the eroding banks have silted in the once-deep holes and destroyed the gravel beds that are essential for insects and trout. Bank erosion, in turn, begins to widen the stream, leading to sedimentation from runoff because of the lack of a buffer zone. The stream continues to widen, and pools and riffles start to be covered up by fine silt. Now the spring creek slowly warms up because of the loss of weed beds, and soon spawning areas, habitats, and insects are lost. The once-thriving spring creek is now in jeopardy of never recovering.

Most of these spring creeks flow through farmlands that have been worked right to edge of the stream. In these instances, fencing the stream can help prevent erosion. Livestock can still use the stream through cattle-crossing areas built with rock to prevent mud and silt from being stomped in the stream. One close example of just how good this works is not that far away from Chambersburg, Pennsylvania, on Cove Creek, which is a great trout stream flowing south out of McConnellsburg. Much of the upper portions were not fenced in at all. Cattle had free access to the small springs entering Cove Creek, and many times the stream would be cloudy because of the cattle tromping through the spring feeders. Once the spring feeders were fenced, Cove Creek soon became less silty and cooler in summer. There is still much more to do, but things are looking up for this woodland fishery.

Spring creeks are threatened by human encroachment. Farms are turning into housing developments with manicured lawns stretching right up to the stream banks. Mowing the grasses prevents the vegetation from stabilizing the stream's fragile banks. Just leaving one foot of uncut grass along the stream can help to stabilize the stream's edge. The tall grass also hosts all kinds of insects. Pesticides can enter the stream and settle into the substrate, which harms insect life. Herbicides are used on the lawns, and they, too, enter the stream and destroy the vital weed beds needed for both trout and insects.

The problems begin well before the houses are built along the streams. The use of explosives can dramatically change the rock formations below the bulldozed meadows. The blasting of rock can change how the water flows through rock formations. Sometimes it can be as little as changing how quickly the water rises out of the rock and as dramatic as wiping out the spring source completely. Unfortunately, I have witnessed a good spring creek fade away due to blasting. This little spring creek used to run full and cool all year. Now, come summer, much of the water has found another path.

So what can be done? Are spring creeks in fact facing a losing battle? The answer is no. Unfortunately, many nice spring creeks have fallen from grace, but many are also being restored by volunteers who want to give something back to the ecosystem. All across the nation, groups are rallying to save and restore spring creeks and many other streams as well. Take a look at the legendary Falling Spring Branch in Chambersburg, Pennsylvania. Many areas of the stream were once wide and flat.

Urban development is encroaching on the banks of these highly sensitive streams.

Despite years of abuse, many spring creeks are holding their own, providing special fishing experiences for wild trout.

Above: Early morning in Fox's Meadow, named for Letort regular, Charlie Fox. If it was not for concerned anglers before us, many spring creeks may be lost today. These conservation-minded pioneers paved the way for us to continue past and present efforts to save these treasured streams. We have to do our part to protect these places for future generations. Left: Charles K. Fox, the Dean of the Letort, was an ardent conservationist.

Concerned fly fishermen formed the Falling Spring Greenway (FSG) and the Falling Spring Trout Unlimited Chapter (FSTU) after watching a once-healthy stream falter. With the grace of the landowners, efforts to restore the stream began in the mid-1970s. The FSTU and FSG soon requested and received grants from the state's Fish and Boat Commission and from Growing Greener.

FSG also approach Guilford Township and established a township ordinance that basically states that if any land along the Falling Spring Branch is sold and subdivided, a public right-of-way must be placed in the land transfer. To this day, the ordinance is responsible for over 90 percent of public access in the stream flowing through Guilford Township.

The process was a long one, but twenty years later, the stream is on the rebound. Ecotone, Inc., was hired to do much of the stream restoration work, including narrowing the stream, root wad placements, and adding lunker structures. When their equipment left, no one could tell the stream had been worked on. Now, Falling Spring can disperse the silt correctly and keep the stream channel clean. Also, thanks to caring landowners, most of the stream is lined by at least a fifteen-foot buffer and sometimes entire meadows that grow wild with vegetation and trees. When they are not mowed down, the wild grasses help stabilize the banks.

Many spring creeks other than the Falling Spring are receiving this same attention. When Beaver Creek, a quaint Maryland spring creek, was in jeopardy, concerned landowners and local fly fishermen organized the Beaver Creek Watershed Association, Inc. (BCWA). They set out to restore and preserve the watershed, and now this once-fallen stream is beginning to get nice hatches and a substantial population of trout.

Thanks in part to concerned anglers, conservation groups, and landowners, the list of restored streams is growing. Hopefully, this trend will continue. Spring creeks will always be threatened, but people have stepped up to save these valuable fisheries from agricultural and industrial pollution, and the most unfortunate no-trespassing signs.

Thanks to concerned anglers, conservation groups, and landowners, the list of restored spring creeks is growing.

Index